WHAT'S BETTER TODAY?

How to Grow and Learn into the Leader You Can Be

DR. JOHN KENWORTHY

PARTRIDGE

A Penguin Random House Company

To order additional copies of this book, contact
Toll Free 800 101 2657 (Singapore)
Toll Free 1 800 81 7340 (Malaysia)
orders.singapore@partridgepublishing.com

www.partridgepublishing.com/singapore

CONTENTS

Part Two—Learn and Grow

Part Three—Wrapping Up

HOW TO GROW AND LEARN INTO THE LEADER YOU CAN BE

Imagine that you are stressed out, overworked, overly pressured and don't get the recognition you deserve. This may be so close to reality that you won't find it hard to imagine! You want to grow in your career, but trapped by your current lifestyle and there's a genuine fear that you may be close to burning out. One day, a friend mentions that she has been helped by a coach and suggests that you do the same. At first, you resist. You've seen the hundreds of articles and adverts promising a silver bullet solution to organise your life, reach your dreams, orchestrate your career and get on top of your life.

So let's get this out of the way now: **There are no silver bullets; no quick and easy solutions; it will not happen overnight.**

You are looking for a coach, so how do you make sure that you get the most out of it?

There are times in life and work when we would benefit from the experience, wisdom and knowledge of people who have been in similar situations. If you are looking for one such person, then you are looking for a coach. Most coaches are professionals, people with considerable experience in one or more sectors, more often than not trained in coaching skills. They choose to become coaches as they are willing to help others by sharing their experience and by helping their coachees to find solutions to their issues, following them through a plan of action.

- According to a report published by CIPD (Chartered Institute of Personnel Development), one in five chief executives claim that having had a coach was critical for their success[1].

Young graduates report to have found their feet in the organisation thanks to the help of their most experienced colleagues. Even people coming up to retirement have been eased through this difficult stage of their life working with people who have "been there before". Within a work environment there are many situations where the help of a coach would be appropriate.

Typical Situations

Most people who seek coaching for themselves are going through (or about to embark on) a transition in their life.

- Taking on a new role or responsibility, or starting in a new industry where you have little experience, but need to gain the skills and experience quickly.
- Starting in a new job/position when you are expected to hit the ground running.
- When needing a personal assessment to determine your strengths and weaknesses, and consider what you should be doing to maximise your potential.
- When striving for promotion or a new position.
- When needing to talk through your thought processes, strategies, and plans to move forward.

---

[1] ANDERSON, V., RAYNER, C. and SCHYNS, B. (2009) Coaching at the sharp end: the role of line managers in coaching at work. Research report. London: Chartered Institute of Personnel and Development.

- When struggling with certain skills and performance areas and you wish to improve.
- When feeling you have reached a plateau in your career and want to explore options.
- Organisations sponsored coaching tend to use external coaches for their more senior leaders and internal coaches for more junior staff. Fortunately, many organisations are realising the benefits of coaching to strengthen and enhance good performance, a few still think of coaching as a last resort to "fix issues".

Are you ready for coaching?

Take our quick assessment and find out how ready you are for coaching now.

http://gainmore.net/cri

THE THREE PHASE OF A COACHING RELATIONSHIP

As time passes, the coaching relationship will find its own balance as coach / coachee will get to know each other. Effective communication and good feedback are the keys to make it work and to ensure that time is used both effectively and efficiently. Every coaching relationship goes through three phases over time, and this guide book is divided into the three parts of these phases:

Starting Out, Learn and Grow and Wrapping Up:

Part One—Starting Out

- Initial contact
- Building rapport
- Defining objectives
- Clarifying roles
- Setting goals
- Discussing mentoring Agreement

Part Two—Learn and Grow

- Developing the relationship
- Process of goal setting, action planning, implementing and reviewing
- Taking decisions
- Problem solving
- Development and growth of both parties

Part Three—Wrapping Up

- Evaluation of process
- Acknowledgement of contribution
- Closure and celebration
- Redefinition of the relationship
- Monitoring and reviewing

Continuous monitoring and reviewing

Monitoring and reviewing the relationship should be done at regular intervals to evaluate how the relationship is progressing. Ideally, during a 12-month programme the reality check should be done at least every 3 months or so.

Reviewing the relationship acts as a reminder to both parties of its goals and addresses any difficulties. This fine-tuning exercise is good practice and improves the relationship.

Useful Questions

- What do I think about my coach?
- What is working well and why?
- Is there anything that can be improved?
- Are we communicating effectively?
- How can we improve the communication?
- Can we optimize the time we spend together?
- What changes should we consider making so that things work better?
- What are we spending too much time or too little time on?

If the coachee is keeping a learning log or a diary (something I cannot recommend enough!) it should be easy to identify the main outcomes and the learning points. It should also be easy to establish the stage of the coaching relationship.

Some programmes run for a set period of time and are related to specific outcomes. However, the coachee may wish to terminate the relationship because the objectives have been achieved. The coachee may also wish to terminate earlier for the opposite reason. This is when coach /coachee do not work well together, causing the relationship to come to a halt. Whilst a discussion should take place between coachee and coach, the programme co-ordinator should also be advised so that a replacement may be found.

Concluding the relationship

A more formal review should take place at the end of the programme, irrespective of whether the goals have been achieved or not. This is an opportunity to reflect on the results, celebrate successes, recognise learning. The important thing is that the relationship ends with positive feelings on both sides.

The end of the programme does not mean the end of the relationship. Many couples continue working together, meeting perhaps less frequently and more informally.

Very often it is at this point that many coachees consider passing on the knowledge and skills they gained by becoming coaches and entering into a new relationship.

ACKNOWLEDGEMENTS

Whilst I may be the author of this book in that I typed the words and somehow pulled it together, it is done with tremendous help of many people, some who knew they were helping and many who did not.

First of all I want to thank my coaching clients. You are the reason I love to go to work each day and without you I would not have learned what I needed to learn to even consider writing this.

To my Professional Leadership Caddy team for their advice and inputs. In particular, Professor A. Lee Gilbert, David Bloch, Terrence Choo, Anne Manning and Sharon Tan—your precious input and ideas on early drafts has been invaluable.

To my beloved wife, Annie, your love and presence in my life and encouragement through the many dark times is my constant. Thank you for putting up with me and challenging me when I needed it.

To my Lord and Saviour, Jesus Christ, You gave me utterance.

PART ONE

STARTING OUT

Part One—Starting Out

Part one of this guide book is about the initial phase of any coaching relationship.

By reading this I already know that you are either seeking help in achieving a specific objective or you are facing a challenge and want some guidance. In this part you'll learn if you are truly ready for coaching, and if so, what type of coaching is going to be most helpful for you right now. Even if you can coach yourself. In fact, by using the templates and guidance in this book, you will be coaching yourself.

In this part, you'll prepare yourself for change and establish your own motivation to persist in making this change happen. You'll know how to choose a coach to partner with you and be ready to play your part in making the relationship work. You'll look at what you really want to achieve through coaching and understand why having clear goals and vision is so important to achieve sustainable success that you want through your coaching.

You'll also know what to expect from your coach, and what your coach will expect from you and be aware of the formal agreement standards that are likely to apply to your relationship with your coach.

And by going through this, you will save yourself time and probably money by being well prepared to ask any potential coach the right questions. And if you find that you have the self-discipline and persistence within yourself, perhaps you won't need someone else to coach you at all.

Do you need a coach?

"Making a decision is only the beginning of things. When someone makes a decision, he is really diving into a strong current that will carry him to places he had never dreamed of when he first made the decision." Paulo Coelho, The Alchemist

Do you need a coach?

"Everybody needs a coach", that's what Professor David Clutterbuck stated back in 1985[1] when coaching, as a management technique, started to spread across the world.

---

[1]   Clutterbuck, David, 2004, Everyone Needs a Mentor. CIPD Publishing.

And I completely agree. If anything, in the quarter century since, the increasing demands on everybody to perform, show their emotional intelligence and cope with the stress of modern living in a healthy way has become more critical. And having a coach can help you do that.

So just what can a coach do for you?

A coach can help you:

- **Gain insight**—particularly about how current behaviour is PERCEIVED by others through providing feedback and assessment.
- **Get clarity of purpose**—Extroverted people who are outer directed (and rewarded behaviours in this world) tend to get their self-esteem from satisfying others' expectations of them. This may cause them to lose touch with what is truly important for themselves. Without clarity of purpose, you may tend to rush through days not knowing what you want to achieve. Often asking what others want rather than seeming to have opinions of their own. Reflection and review through coaching can help here.
- **Help you improve relationships**—changing behaviours in relationships changes their perception of the other party and you'll get more open and honest feedback. Coaching that helps you conduct planned conversations with colleagues is especially useful here.
- **Broaden your perspectives**—we all play a role and have a preference of the way we process . . . . increasing the diversity of opinions we consider in decisions broadens our perspective leading to improved and more acceptable decisions.

- **Develop your leadership skills**—developing the skills each individual needs for their new position or a future role.
- **Help you identify and overcome barriers to change** change occurs over time, unlearning is often resisted, especially deeply rooted habits, and stress causes us to revert to preference. Self-righteousness is often the biggest barrier. Coaching can identify and discuss the roadblocks developing strategies and new ways of thinking to overcome them.
- **Improve your ability to learn**—dependence on your coach for feedback is a disservice. Internalizing the ability to learn and continuously grow, sustaining behaviour and results. Coaching uses a cyclical process, making this process explicit, the coachee becomes more skilled at using the same process on their own.

When is Coaching needed?

There are times in life and work when we would benefit from the experience, wisdom and knowledge of people who have been in similar situations. If you are looking for one such person, then you are looking for a coach. Most coaches are professionals, people with considerable experience in one or more sectors, more often than not trained in coaching skills. They choose to become coaches as they are willing to help others by sharing their experience and by helping their coachees to find solutions to their issues, following them through a plan of action.

According to a report published by CIPD (Chartered Institute of Personnel Development), one in five chief executives claim that having had a coach was critical for their success[2].

Young graduates report to have found their feet in the organisation thanks to the help of their most experienced colleagues. Even people coming up to retirement have been eased through this difficult stage of their life through people who have "been there before". Within a work environment there are many situations where the help of a coach would be appropriate.

Typical Situations when having a coach will really help you

- Starting in a new job/position when you are expected to hit the ground running.
- Taking on a new role or responsibility, or starting in a new industry where you have little experience, but need to gain the skills and experience quickly.
- When needing a personal assessment to determine your strengths and weaknesses, and consider what you should be doing in order to maximise your potential.
- When striving for promotion or a new position.
- When needing to talk through your thought processes, strategies, and plans in order to move forward.
- When struggling with certain skills and performance areas and you wish to improve.
- When feeling you have reached a plateau in your career and want to explore options.

---

[2] *ANDERSON, V., RAYNER, C. and SCHYNS, B. (2009) Coaching at the sharp end: the role of line managers in coaching at work. Research report. London: Chartered Institute of Personnel and Development.*

Can I do this without a coach?

To a certain extent, yes. That's exactly what this book is about. It takes a certain amount of self-discipline and you'll need to set yourself targets to achieve and the tenacity to keep on keeping on.

Use the templates here and you'll be working on the same things that 80% of our clients find most useful in their first coaching season. The other 20%? Well, those are things that need a coach.

A word of warning

You will have blockages and defences (we all have them), and you will have particular heuristics in thinking (mental short-cuts) that have developed over your life. You may not even know about them. So when you encounter resistance with yourself, most typically you'll procrastinate about actually doing the template, make a note and pledge yourself to push through regardless. If you still find yourself resisting . . . get a professional coach to help you.

Am I ready for Coaching? Assessment

Am I ready for coaching? Assessment http://gainmore.net/wbt-ready

Questions and objections to beingcoached:

- **I'm already successful, why do I need a coach?**
  - When does an athlete get a coach, when they're not very good or when they are already performing well? How much more successful could you be if you had a coach?
- **Since I'm reading this and it looks to me as if I can just use this to coach myself?**
  - Yes, absolutely right, you can coach yourself. So long as you have the self-discipline to ensure that you do it and the ability to recognise your own baggage and blockages (believe me, we all have some) and deal with them.
- **But isn't coaching for people who have "real problems"?**
  - No. True counselling, psychologists and psychiatrists—fully qualified medical practitioners —handle such cases.
- **OK, for those who aren't performing well then?**
  - Coaching would possibly benefit them, though it's rarely the best investment.
- **Aren't most coaches just people who don't have a real job?**
  - A little harsh, but for some this is true. Many coaches are individuals who have left (voluntarily or otherwise) the corporate world and coaching is seen as an easy way to make money and have a decent work/life balance. They have knowledge and

expertise and, increasingly, qualifications to be a coach. Some qualifications are rigorous, others less so. And being qualified does not make you a "good" coach. I suggest you look at their longevity as a coach and real testimonials from real clients (Linked In references are a good indicator—at least there's an authenticated user who has posted it). Oh, and it's not an "easy" way to make money, but yes the work/life balance can be excellent and doing what I love and getting paid for it . . .

- **Doesn't a coach have to be older/more senior/more successful than I?**
  - No. You are the one with the resources and answers. Your coach is the person who helps you find and leverage those resources you have.
- **But I don't want some young, inexperienced person as my coach . . .**
  - Then don't hire them.
- **Don't they need to know my business or industry?**
  - If you want to improve in a technical competence (a job skill) yes.
- **Shouldn't my company provide coaching for me?**
  - If you won't invest in you, why should they?
- **Isn't coaching expensive?**
  - In terms of time and commitment, yes. In terms of money—yes if you hire someone really well-known and even famous. Think in terms of investment and know what return you want.

What's the difference between Coaching, Mentoring, Counselling and Managing?

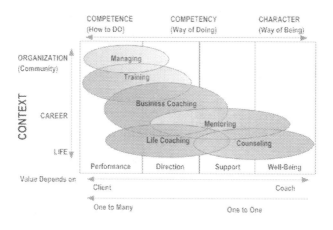

"There are painters who transform the sun to a yellow spot, but there are others who transform a yellow spot into the sun" Pablo Picasso

What's the difference between coaching, mentoring, counselling, training and managing?

Let's, however, take a look at the main similarities and differences, as this may be helpful for you in establishing the style you would prefer someone works with you.

There is considerable overlap between these development approaches with each having a performance, direction, support or personal well-being focus in the context of the organisation, your career or your whole life.

Improving performance is largely about developing your job skills (competences). Whilst developing your soft skills (competencies) is better served through direction and support. Developing your character is best served through supporting your development and a focus on your personal well-being.

You will see that there are overlaps indicated in the diagram. Perhaps more so with the growth of 'life coaching' which has filled a niche in developing you in your life whilst not being therapy or counselling.

What is mentoring?

In spite of its origins in Greek culture some 3,000 years ago, mentoring is a buzzword today where life and work is high-tech but not high-touch.

When we use the word "mentoring", a dozen or more different images race across our minds. It seems that we might not all be on the same page. It will serve us well then, to offer a working definition that brings us all together in our understanding. Here, I have tweaked a definition original from Paul Stanley and Robert Clifton[1] and later by Dr. Tim Elmore[2]:

> *Mentoring is a working relational experience through which one person empowers and enables another by sharing their wisdom and resources.*

What is coaching?

In the 16th century, the word 'coach' described a horse-drawn vehicle to take people from where they were to where they wanted to be. In the 20th century, big buses with rows of seats were also called coaches, and their purpose was the same: to get people to where they wanted to go. The word 'coach' was given

---

[1]   Stanley, Paul D. et el, 1994, Mentoring.
[2]   Tim Elmore, 2009, Life Giving Mentors. Growing Leaders.

athletic meaning around when it was used to identify the person who tutored university students in their rowing on the Cam River in Cambridge. Later, the word (and role) became associated with musicians, public speakers and actors, who rely on coaches to improve their skills. Don Shula, former coach for the Miami Dolphins, wrote about athletes who would come to his team with their skills and talents, ready to submit to the coach whose job was to instruct, discipline, and inspire them to do things better than they thought they could do on their own. Over time, the idea of a coach has not really changed. A coach is a vehicle to take someone from where they are now, to where they want to be. Eric Parsloe, author of "The Manager as Coach and Mentor"[3] defines coaching as:

"a process that enables learning and development to occur and thus performance to improve."

The table below is an overview of the main differences between the four most common approaches to coaching and how these differ from the manager's role.

Focus	receiving instruction and guidance	receiving structured support to find own solutions to issues	giving and receiving direction and counselling options	psychological well-being	giving instruction and direction
Context	community and the organisation or team	the individual's job & work	personal development for future career and life	well understanding to adopt more constructive life practices	tasks to be done within the role and development for career within team
Orientation	discussion	probing	application	discussion	skill transfer
Number	ten to fifteen	one-on-one to one-on-eight	one-on-one to one-on-three	one-on-one	one-on-one to one-on-twenty
Value depends on:	attendees learning and transfer	the coach's skills and the coachee's motivation	the mentor's experience and knowledge & psychological willingness to share	the experience and psychological training of the skill in question	the manager's authority & skill recognition
Content	based on the leader	based on needs of the job	based on needs of the mentee	based on the needs of the client	based on task needs
Goal	goal is collective	performance improvement	intentional growth / investment	personal well-being	job skill development / need task efficiency
Progress	often sporadic	depends on motivation	made by pre-determined goals	depends on severity of issues	depends on skills
Level of Accountability	low level	mid to high level	high, intense level	mid-level	intense level
Method	community (Heart and Mind)	question and probing (will and mind)	direction and leadership (heart, will and mind)	either emphasis on behaviour, on thinking and/or on emotional aspects.	motivation and management (mind)
Purpose	to meet and interact and increase knowledge	to improve performance in role	to reach potential in career and life	personal well-being	efficiency and effectiveness within correct role.

---

3   Eric Parsloe, 1999, *Manager As Coach & Mentor*. CIPD Publishing.

Review the table in detail

Comparing Coaching, Mentoring, Counselling and Managing

http://gainmore.net/wbt-compare

All of these approaches are processes by which people are taken from where they are (their skills, talents, knowledge, position) to where they want to be. Throughout this book, we refer to the ubiquitous term "coaching" to refer to any non-therapeutic development activity that may cross these boundaries of teaching, coaching, mentoring or counselling.

Coaching is about change

"There are no such things as wrong turns, Only paths we never knew we were supposed to take." Proverb

It's all about change

"Change is the only constant" goes the refrain. There would be little need for coaching, training, mentoring, counselling or any development if people were happy to stay the same as they are now.

Being coached by someone is all about being empowered, equipped and enabled to change. Coaching empowers people to find new jobs, work though transitions, enhance performance, build better relationships, make wise decisions, transform organisations and reach new spiritual levels. Coaching is about establishing a vision of the future and reaching goals. When coaching is successful, it's about bringing and maintaining change.

But coaching is more. We also help people determine what needs to stay the same in times of constant flux. We encourage our clients to stake out their core values, established strengths, basic beliefs, ethical principles and lasting relationships that remain firm and provide an anchor to their lives.

Coaches are both change agents and constant agents. Coaches help people see what needs to change and what needs to remain constant.

Change is difficult!

Let's start by recognising the obvious: change is difficult. Going on a journey with people through change can be challenging and exhausting. Bringing sustainable change is even harder. Most people resist change even when they see the need and believe it can occur.

The owner of the first hotel I managed was just 40 when he suffered a heart attack. His lifestyle, booze, food and a lack of regular exercise were contributory factors but prior to the heart attack, there were no significant symptoms. Life was good, then BAM! He was on the floor in agony. He survived. His doctor told him bluntly that he had to change his diet, give up alcohol, smoking and take up regular exercise. Change or die! A stark choice. And one that many people face. Initially, my boss came out of hospital ready and eager to take this advice seriously and changed everything that was harming his health. It wasn't easy for him, but he stuck with it and now enjoys a slim, healthy life retired and sailing around the Mediterranean.

Yet, in the US alone, some 90% of heart bypass patients can't change their lifestyles, even at the risk of dying. It's not surprising then that changing people's behaviour in business is a challenge.

How people face change

People respond to change typically in four different ways depending on their personalities and past experiences:

- **Innovators**—who value change and often try to make it happen.
- **Embracers**—who thrive on change and accept it with enthusiasm, sometimes without thinking too much about it.
- **Acceptors**—who initially resist change but eventually go along with it because there is no alternative.
- **Resisters**—who may not even notice the change, deliberately ignore it, or be so overwhelmed that they push it out of their awareness. Some even deny any need for change and refuse to budge an inch.

People usually lean towards one of these responses. There's some excellent news though: simply because you are reading this, you are likely to be an innovator or embracer. If you are reading this reluctantly, you're an acceptor. And those who aren't reading this . . . well, they're the resisters (but of course they won't know that because they didn't read it!).

Motivation to change

"If you limit your choices only to what seems possible or reasonable, you disconnect yourself from what you truly want, and all that is left is a compromise." Robert Fitz

Change is uncomfortable

As you embark on any learning and growth journey we will be asking you to use tools and techniques that you are unfamiliar with. Sometimes, these techniques make you feel uncomfortable, because they are new and it 'feels' different. We ask that you persevere with using the techniques—this is not a quick fix. Just as you don't expect to visit the gym once and come out with the body of an Adonis—change takes work. Some of this 'work' may feel uncomfortable for a while.

Let's try a real simple change that is uncomfortable.

- As you sit there, please cross your arms.
- Now, as you sit there with your arms crossed, you are relaxed and at ease.

- Now, swap your arm crossing to the opposite way. If you normally cross your arms left over right, change it to right over left. Tuck the other hand in . . .
- Are you comfortable?
- You still have your arms crossed, yet it feels a little uncomfortable.
- How many times would you have to deliberately change the way you cross your arms until this too is comfortable? 5, 10, 20, 30 times?
- Now, consider that some of the tools and techniques that we will be introducing to you may feel a little uncomfortable to begin with. But just like your arm crossing, with perseverance and repeated use, these new ways of behaving for you will become comfortable.

Remember, change occurs over time, and unlearning is often resisted, especially deeply rooted habits, and stress causes us to revert to preference.

It will help you greatly to find your own motivation to change. The reason and pay off that will make the effort worthwhile.

Motivation is a fruit

This is a critical understanding that few people realise. Motivation is the fruit of actions towards a goal that satisfy a personal value. We feel motivated **after the fact**. However, we can generate the feeling of motivation by linking the resources we shall be using (time, effort, money, skills, knowledge) to the achievement of a specific outcome and linking this to the anticipated personal value that the achievement of this outcome will bring.

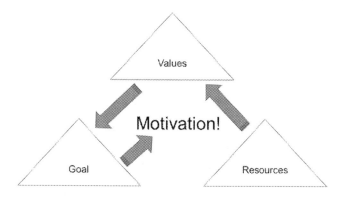

Through coaching you are embarking on a journey of change. Change in your mindset, your attitude, your perceptions and or your behaviours.

- The goal is the specific change you want to achieve
- The resources are things like your time and effort, and maybe other costs. For example in changing your attitude about another person—you will lose the previous relationship and gain a different relationship with that individual.
- Values are what's important for you. This could be as simple as feeling successful because you've chosen to make a change and done what was necessary. It may be something longer term, such as a new position or the feeling of accomplishment.

The feeling of motivation to change comes from linking these three in your mind.

We're going to use a template here to guide you through this. If this is your first time going through this book, start with something simple but important. You've started reading this for a good reason. There's something that you believe will bring benefit to you. So we'll start with completing this book as the outcome we want.

Step 1—Establish the unwanted behaviour

- Now, how much time each week have you been spending on your personal development?
- How much time are you going to spend from now until you complete this book? (Hint, this number of hours should be higher, yet still reasonable.)
- Thus the unwanted behaviour is your 'old' commitment in time (and effort) to personal development.
- Write this down specifically, with numbers and details, for yourself in the template.

Step 2—Now, let's establish a broad overview of your long, medium and short-term goals.

- Your short-term goal is to complete this book.
  - What time frame are you putting on this? 3 weeks, 6, 12?
- What do you want to achieve in your career or business in the medium term?
  - What's the time frame for this 'medium term' for you?
- What about your long-term goal for your career or business, say 5 to 10 years from now?

Write down your answers in the template.

Step 3—Why are these goals important for you?

- Read your long-term goal out loud and ask yourself "What is the purpose of achieving this long-term goal for me?"

- What other purpose do I have for achieving this goal?
- And, what other purpose do I have for achieving this goal?

Write down your answers in the values column.

Now repeat this for your medium term goal.

Lastly, your short-term goal of completing this book.

- What is the purpose, for you, that you complete this book within the time you specified?
- And what other purpose do you have for completing this book?
- And what additional purpose do you have for completing this book?

Write down all your answers in the values column.

Discover at least 3 different values from yourself. Value1, Value2, Value3,

Now answer the following question?

> *"So when you no longer unwanted behaviour you will be more/have more etc value1, value2, value3 . . . is that so?"*

Link changing the unwanted behaviour to the values, for example:

So, when you no longer procrastinate you will be more successful, have more time with your family and be able to earn more money, is that so?

Now, let's find out what you do want instead of your unwanted behaviour:

> *"As you do not want this unwanted behaviour, what is that you do want that is not the unwanted behaviour?"*

Because I know that you can follow instructions, you now have a feeling that is very like motivation. Share your completed template with someone who cares about you. This will add another motivation for you because then you will also be accountable (and I already know that you value being thought of as responsible and accountable for your own life.)

Use the Generating Motivation to Change Template

Motivation to Change Template http://gainmore.net/wbt-mtc

Choosing a Coach

"I'm looking for a mentor who can show me how to succeed
Without actually having to do any work."

How do you choose a coach?

There's no absolutes when it comes to choosing a coach to work with. And there's no universal accreditation body or standards that can be relied upon. In fact, at the time of writing at least, there's no legislation anywhere in the world that requires someone to have any specific training or certification to call themselves a coach. It's very much a case of "buyer beware" and up to you to do the research.

Here are some general guidelines to help you choose:

- It is useful for them to have a degree in business, psychology or organisational behaviour. A graduate degree may be preferable.
- Specialised training can supplement an educational background. Coaches should have specific training (and certification) for the psychological instruments they use.

- Some experience as managers or executives. The best experience is a lot of practice in coaching various individuals in diverse organisations.
- Accreditation by any coaching body (ICF, AOEC, COC and many others) is no guarantee of quality coaching.

In addition, ask yourself if your coach needs technical experience in my industry? Most managers believe their industry or business is unique. That you organisational culture is different. This is rarely the case. A skilled coach can figure out the norms, language and values fairly quickly. Technical experience or knowledge is only suitable if this is the area in which you need to develop skills and knowledge.

- Should personality match or mismatch influence the selection of a coach?
  - Sometimes, differences help. Sometimes, similarities help (it increases the chance of empathy)
- Male or female?
  - Would the coach's gender make a difference in your comfort level? If so, it matters. If not, it doesn't.
  - If any of your coaching issues have to do with how you relate to men or women, then coaching could be a useful laboratory.

Download the Coaching Style Indicator Assessment

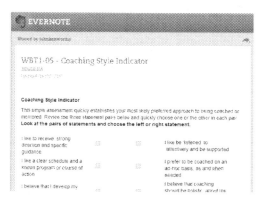

Coaching Style Indicator http://gainmore.net/wbt-style

Building rapport with your coach

Can I borrow your spectacles, it helps me see the world from your perspective

"For us to have the same partnership, I cannot begin a conversation when I am suppressed. I have to approach it with my barriers lifted. I have to give myself to the closeness and want to be what arises from it." Hugh Prather, Notes to myself.

Building rapport with your coach

Coaching is essentially a relationship between two individuals; therefore it is of utmost importance that a rapport is established between you. The first meeting, particularly if it is face to face, can be a bit daunting for some coachees. Organisations wishing to have some control over the programme and the relationships may ask the coaches / coachees to either meet in a social context pre-arranged by the company / organisation or use a facilitator to guide the pair through the process.

More often than not though, the pair will decide when and where to meet. The first meeting is crucial; it is about getting to know each other, seeing whether the chemistry works, finding commonalities and establishing the ground rules by going through the coaching agreement.

Typical agenda for the first meeting

- Introductions (background, experience, common interests)
- Ground rules (what is acceptable and what is not)
- Objectives (for the meeting and for the relationship)
- Review of the coachee's current situation and personal SWOT analysis
- Discussion on learning styles
- When, where and how often to meet
- Any cost involved and contractual agreements
- Actions (things to be done before the next meeting)
- Date of next meeting

If the first meeting works, then the pair will continue to meet, being mindful and respectful of what was agreed. Having a structure to follow for the meetings help the pair with preparation, for building confidence in each other and for having a productive relationship.

Working one-to-one with an experienced professional coach can help you to shorten your learning curve and give you the advantage you need to get that promotion, negotiate and close a deal, gain a competitive advantage, give you the confidence and assurance to take the next step, or just help you to be happier and more satisfied in life.

The success of the coaching relationship depends in part on the skills, knowledge and values of the participants. Coachees need to access their emotional intelligence in order to move the relationship to a deeper and meaningful level. They also need to buy in on the values of coaching and its potential benefits.

Develop your rapport-building skills

I Colour I Listen—Developing Rapport-Building Skills
http://gainmore.net/wbt-icolour

Growth Mindset

Carol Dweck's excellent book on Mindset[1] shows us that there are two dominant mindsets that people choose to believe of themselves and about learning and growth. Anyone who is involved in any learning and growth will recognize these two mindsets. The Mindset diagram[2] represents the two types of mindsets and I'll sure you'll recognize the attitudes of many people you know.

Growth Mindset

Let's first take a look at the **Growth Mindset**:

---

[1]   Mindset: The New Psychology of Success, Carol S. Dweck, 2006 Random House, New York
[2]   http://gainmore.net/wbt-mindset

Growth Mindset

Intelligence can be developed

Leads to a desire to learn and therefore a tendency to:

Individuals who hold the **Growth Mindset** believe that intelligence can be and is developed, that the brain is like a muscle that can be trained. With this belief is the desire to improve.

Embrace challenges

Challenges

To improve, firstly you embrace challenges, because you know that overcoming challenges makes you stronger.

Persist in the face of setbacks

Obstacles

No matter what you decide to do, there will be obstacles. For the Growth Mindset believer, external setbacks do not discourage you. Your self-esteem and self-image are not tied to how you look to others or your success. You see failure as the best opportunity to learn, thus, either way, you win.

See effort as the
path to mastery  Effort

You don't see effort as something useless to be avoid but as *necessary* to grow and master useful skills.

Learn from
criticism  Criticism

No-one truly enjoys criticism or negative feedback but the Growth Mindset individual integrates feedback that has genuine worth as an opportunity to change and learn. Negative feedback is not seen as a personal attack, but for what it is; feedback.

Find lessons and
inspiration in the
success of others Success of Others

The success of others is seen as a source of inspiration and information. To **Growth Mindset** individuals, success is not seen as a zero-sum game (http://gainmore.net/zero-sum).

As a result, they reach higher levels of achievement

All this gives them a greater sense of free will

Growth Mindset individuals will improve because of this, and this creates positive feedback loops that encourages them to keep learning, growing and improving.

Fixed Mindset

Let's have a look at the **Fixed Mindset** side:

Fixed Mindset

Intelligence
Static

Leads to a desire to look smart and therefore a tendency to:

Those who hold these beliefs think that "they are the way they are". This doesn't mean that they have any less desire for a positive self-image than anyone else and they do want to perform well and look smart. But, to achieve these goals . . .

Challenges   Avoid challenges

Challenge is hard and success is not assured, so rather than risk failing and negatively impacting their self-image, they will often avoid challenges and stick to what they know they can do well.

Obstacles   Give up easily

Obstacles face everyone but the difference with the Fixed Mindset individual is that obstacles are seen as external forces that get in the way and are either avoided (leading to sub-optimal results and usually, blaming others) or are the 'excuse' for giving up.

Effort   See effort as
                                                   fruitless or
                                                   worse

When effort is required and your view is that effort is unpleasant and rarely pays dividends . . . what's the point in exerting that effort? The smart thing to do then is avoid as much effort as possible.

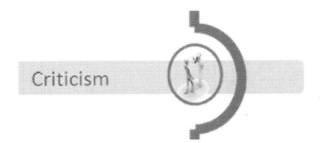

Negative feedback tends to be ignored because the **Fixed Mindset** leads you to believe that any criticism of your capabilities is criticism of *you*. This is discouraging to the people who are giving you feedback and after a while they stop giving any negative feedback, further isolating the person from external influences that could generate some change.

Other's success is used as a benchmark to beat yourself with. Success, in this worldview is put down to luck or unprincipled actions. Some will go further and deride another person's success finding juicy gossip to attach to them when their success is being lauded by anyone else.

> As a result, they may plateau early and achieve less than their full potential
> All this confirms their deterministic view of the world

The results is that they don't reach their full potential and their beliefs feed on themselves: They don't change or improve much with time, if at all, and so to them this confirms that "they are as they are".

What Now?

The good news—especially if you just recognized yourself as being someone who holds the **Fixed Mindset** worldview—is that it is possible to change from one to the other.

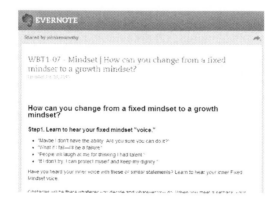

Changing from Fixed to Growth Mindset—
Exercise http://gainmore.net/wbt-change

Part One—Starting Out

Receiving Feedback

"True friendship is the courage to articulate to people what you really see in them—to tell them of the good and wonderful things you see, as well as the difficult and confrontational." Yaron Golan

Receiving Feedback

Whenever somebody gives you feedback in the normal course of your work or life, it is highly likely that **you** perceive it as negative feedback; meanwhile, they're thinking that it's just feedback for your own good. You feel defensive and possibly upset, because, after all, you're doing your best. Or when you know that you were at fault, you are even more defensive. Yeah. Been there, seen the move, have the t-shirt!

Most people do not give feedback to someone else well. But without feedback, we simply don't know how our actions are perceived.

Receiving feedback is something that most leaders also don't do well. Get into the habit of asking your clients and team members for their feedback and follow these tips:

- Adopt a receptive posture (listen to the feedback as if it were a gift)
- Don't be defensive (listen to the feedback as something to learn from)
- Listen (listen some more)
- Acknowledge (paraphrase and summarise to ensure that you understand correctly)
- Thank (say "Thank you")

Examples of great questions to ask when receiving feedback:

- "Please be more specific"
- "Can you give me another example"
- "I am still unclear why . . ."

After thanking the person giving you feedback, you do NOT need to defend your actions, or give reasons. The best posture to adopt is to decide how you will act from now and inform the other person what you intend.

Yes, I understand, sometimes, feedback is criticism and may even be "unfair" and you do have reasons for behaving as you did. So what? Be the bigger person, and choose to accept the feedback with grace and what you will do with it.

Clarifying Roles

"You have no control over what the other guy does.
You only have control over what you do." A.J. Kitt

The values that underpin coaching are such that responsibilities are shared by everyone involved in the process. Trust, honesty and confidentiality are fundamental for an ethical approach to coaching.

The most important responsibility and role of every coachee is that of making the most of the learning. Without this commitment from you as the coachee, coaching would be pointless.

Every coach will work in their own particular way. Some will allow you to contact them on an ad-hoc basis, others have a strict schedule. Some coaches will "chase" you (aka nag) for updates and progress, others rely on you to manage this yourself. Some provide you a private web-based portal for tracking your progress and reminding you of actions and keeping notes that both of you can access, other coaches don't keep notes. It's up to the coachee to find out and decide what you need from your coach and to work with one that supports you the way you want to be supported.

Defining Expectations

A number of coachees overlook this important aspect of the coaching agreement. Defining expectations and monitoring them on a regular basis is important so as to avoid disappointment and to strengthen the relationship.

Coach's responsibilities:

- Respect confidentiality of all discussions absolutely.
- Be prepared for scheduled and agreed coaching sessions with a clear mind and without distractions.
- Recognise and deal effectively with strong emotions.
- Establish ground rules for session scheduling, venue or systems.
- Push and challenge the coachee in new ways of thinking and performance.
- Agree outcomes, coachee actions and follow through on any offer of resources and support.

Coachee's responsibilities:

- Respecting confidentiality and personal information given by the coach.
- Recognising that the coach's time and energy is precious and that they should be used wisely, taking care to be punctual and to attend the meetings at the given time and place, or at least to give plenty of notice in case of a necessary, but unexpected cancellation.

- Expecting that a coaching process can sometimes cause strong feelings and emotions which should not be used against the coach.
- Be ready to take over the management of the relationship in terms of setting the agenda and defining time and locations for the meetings.
- Be prepared to be challenged and to challenge the coach so as to create an interesting and mutually beneficial dialogue.
- Follow through on actions following your coaching sessions. It is in the application of new behaviours or knowledge that will benefit the coachee.

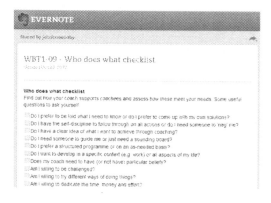

Who does what checklist http://gainmore.net/wbt-check

Defining Objectives

*"I always knew that I'd amount to something.
I guess I should have been more specific"*

*The greater danger for most of us lies not in setting
our aim too high and falling short; but in setting our
aim too low, and achieving our mark." Michelangelo*

What do you want to achieve?

We've seen already that coaching is all about change. But what is
it exactly that you want to change? What do you want to achieve
through coaching?

This is often different to what you want to achieve (in life, work,
career etc.) The latter we will look at in a short while. Right now,
let's focus a few minutes on what you want coaching for.

In my own experience as a coach these past 20 plus years, more
than 70% of my clients had an objective to, well, set an objective.
In other words, they didn't know what they wanted to get out of
coaching, there was just something bothering them and they knew
they needed to change. What to change was another matter.

Indeed, I believe this is one of the reasons for the growth in coaching as a profession.

So let me ask you as if I were currently your coach:

How can I serve you?

What can I do to help you achieve your life/work/ career goals (that you cannot do for yourself)?

I shared in "**Do you need a coach?**" the key things a coach can do for you. In the list below you should be able to identify your needs in an issue around the 10 most prevalent areas of life transition. Beneath each of the main issues you can see the first key objective where a coach may be able to help and what sort of coaching is most suitable:

Issues around

- **Your needs**
  - *General coaching objectives*—most useful coaching approach

Career Development

- **Identify a clear career path and be encouraged to pursue it**
  - *Get clarity of purpose*—Support and Guidance

Starting a new job

- **Quickly assimilating the company culture**
  - *Broaden perspectives*—Learning and build self-confidence

Strengthening capability

- **Improve leadership skills and creative thinking**
  - *Develop leadership skills* and *gain insight* Learning and support

Improving performance

- **Personal growth and better performance**
  - *Improve ability to learn*—Learning and self-confidence

Improving motivation

- **Build on existing knowledge and be committed**
  - *Get clarity of purpose*—Support and self-confidence

Starting a business

- **Being as certain as possible for success**
  - *Gain insight*—Support and advice

Major change in life

- **Decide on a future direction and follow through**
  - *Identify barriers to change*—Learning and support and self-confidence

Relationships

- **Build better and stronger relationships**
  - *Gain insight* and *help improving relationships* Learning intra and interpersonal sensitivity

Decision Making

- **Make better decisions**
  - *Overcome barriers to change*—Learning and self-confidence

"Stuck"

- **Overcome procrastination or poor time management**
  - *Identify barriers to change*—Support, self-confidence and learning

This should help you identify the main help you need right now and better equip you to discuss your unique situation more productively with any potential coach.

Coaching Objectives Checklist Questions http://gainmore.net/wbt obj

Introduction to Metrics

I think it might help to be a little more specific here

"What gets measured gets managed". Peter Drucker

Coaching and Development Metrics

Imagine you are standing in a field with a bow and arrow. In the distance is a target with three concentric rings.

Instantly you know that your goal is to shoot an arrow to hit the target and preferably in the bull's-eye.

You can shoot your arrow and get immediate feedback on how well you achieved your goal . . . or not. If you achieved a bull's-eye, awesome, now you want to consistently do so. If you missed, you can adjust how you shot the last arrow and keep managing what you do until you achieve your goal.

- It's easy and straightforward to measure your own achievement.

Now, imagine yourself in a workplace. You are the leader of the group in that workplace and you want to be a "better leader".

Tell me, how will you know that you have achieved your goal of being a better leader?

Difficult to measure this, isn't it? And if you can't measure it, you can't manage what you do to ensure that you achieve your goal.

Most people don't fail on account of the competition;
most people sabotage themselves. If you don't look
at yourself honestly, then you will never understand
where your personal difficulties lie. John C. Maxwell

And if you cannot see your weak spots, then you will fall victim to them.

So what is a suitable metric?

To be able to measure something you need to be able to see it, hear it, smell it, taste it or touch it. And you need a benchmark to compare it with. "How tall I am in metres or feet and inches" or "how tall am I now compared to last year" (those notches on the doorpost your mum made when you were a child).

It's not always easy to establish suitable metrics for the 'softer' skills such as leadership, so think of the component parts of specifically what you want to do . . . for example:

- I want to more easily influence my boss . . .
    - You might consider the time it takes to influence your boss now . . . and each time you do so.
    - You might consider how many meetings you have, or how many reports, or how many emails . . .

Your metrics may not be an exact measure but we choose those that are the best proxies.

The metrics you decide upon will be milestones along the way to achieving your overall goal for coaching and beyond. Keeping regular track of how you are progressing, I have found with ALL my clients is the surest guarantee of success.

If your coach uses an online support system that provides such metrics then you can easily keep track. Or else, you can use one for yourself (be your own coach and coachee). I use coachaccountable. com (I am an affiliate, by the way) and highly recommend it for both coaches and self-coaching.

The Importance of Vision

"Vision leads the leader. It paints the target. It sparks and fuels the fire within. Show me a leader without vision, and I'll show you someone who isn't going anywhere." John C. Maxwell

Martin Luther King Jr. inspired people from the steps of the Lincoln Memorial because he painted a picture of what the future could be like. Big visions bring big commitments whilst lifting people out of the monotony of their everyday, humdrum lives and put them in a new world filled with opportunity, hope and challenge.

A vision can involve millions of people or it can be very personal.

So why is vision so important?

Imagine you are driving your car down along the autobahn in Germany. One where there are still no speed limits and you have a lot of horses under the power of your right foot.

It's a beautiful, crystal clear day and you can see the road ahead for many miles . . . how fast would you go?

On the other side of a tunnel you whizz through is a thick blanket of fog. You can just about see the end of the car bonnet. The road ahead is straight, well, according to the map it is straight. You haven't seen another vehicle on the road for many miles. So you keep the pedal to the floor and continue on your journey . . . ?

When you can't see where you are going, you slow down.

The same is true in your life, career and business. Without a vision of the future, you will go slower. Indeed, without a vision ahead, you may well be going the wrong way entirely.

But it is not just having a vision. Sorry if you've been sucked in by Rhonda Byrne's "The Secret"—having a vision is critical and so is achieving results. It's simply untrue that all you need to do is dream big dreams about the future and they will happen. You actually do have to do something to achieve them and get results.

And it's worth while planning and organising yourself to get some smaller quick wins early. The more results you get on your journey, the more sustainable your success will be.

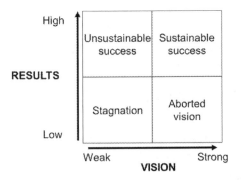

The matrix here shows clearly how vision and results combine to create the success you want. No vision, and no results . . . in theory you stay where you are, in practice you already know, you go backwards. A compelling vision and few results means that you will abort the vision. Good results without a vision will become unsustainable. Only when you have both a big vision and high achievement of results (many small wins), does success become sustainable.

Discussing the Coaching Agreement

"There are only two options regarding commitment. You're either IN or you're OUT. There's no such thing as life in-between." Pat Riley

Setting the terms for the relationship in some detail at an initial face-to-face meeting will make the relationship stronger and more productive. However, agreeing on the terms of the relationship is not merely about drawing up a formal agreement. At the initial meeting there should be an honest and open discussion of backgrounds and experience which will help with building trust and rapport.

Both partners should come to an understanding of why they will be working together, what they want to accomplish and how they are going to reach the desired outcomes.

Here is a checklist of the issues to be discussed at the first meeting. A coaching agreement template is included in this field guide. This agreement can be easily adapted to suit the specifics of any coaching relationship.

How, when and where meetings and communications will occur?

- Lack of time is the reason cited most often for the failure of a coaching relationship. Both coach and coachee need to understand that embarking on a coaching relationship requires a commitment of time. Any concerns should be addressed at this stage and parameters should be set very clearly so as to avoid any disappointments.

The expectations of both coachee and coach?

- A coaching relationship is a two-way relationship; therefore expectations on both sides should be stated and verified at regular intervals.

Logistics of the relationship?

- How, when and where meetings and communications will occur.

How to deal with confidential information?

- Because of the very nature of the relationship, confidentiality and conflicts of interest can be sensitive and complex issues to deal with. This is why it is important to recognize and agree what is to be confidential at the start of any coaching or mentoring relationship.

Which topics or issues are outside the scope of the relationship?

- Professional issues arising in a coaching relationship could include anything from strategy to marketing and networking; from ethical to moral concerns as well as other, more practical issues. Personal issues are often openly disclosed although some companies may discourage this practice. Ultimately, it is up to the coach and coachee to agree what is in and outof-bounds.

How obstacles or problems between the pair are to be dealt with?

- A mismatch may occur and problems may arise during the course of the relationship. In an open and honest relationship these issues could be ironed out, however the pair may agree to refer to the programme coordinator for help if this is arranged by your organisation. Typical issues that tend to arise are: Having two individuals with matching chemistries is not always easy. Coaches and coachees will have to adjust as they find their own coaching styles and preferences. However, they can get a reasonably good idea of how they will get along at the first meeting.
  - Coachees wanting too much time
  - Coachees being too needy
  - Coachees seeking help on issues that are outside the agreed boundaries
  - Total lack of chemistry between the pair

How and when to end the relationship?

- Within a structured coaching programme, there is invariably a beginning and an end. However, some couples may decide to end the relationship ahead of the formal closure when the objectives have been reached or when the relationship has run out of steam or when it needs to be terminated due to unforeseen circumstances. Some relationships on the other hand continue even after the programme has ended. Once again it is up to coach / coachee to agree on this.

What happens during each coaching session?

- Each coach will most likely use a structured framework or 'coaching model' during their sessions. These vary in length and structure and it will help you to know how they approach each session.

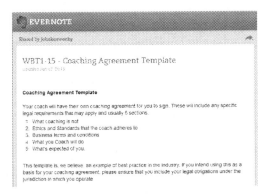

Coaching Agreement template http://gainmore.net/wbt-agree

PART TWO

LEARN AND GROW

Part Two—Learn and Grow

Part two of this guide book is the meat of the coaching partnership.

In here, you will benefit from preparing thoroughly for working with your coach and saving you oodles of time. More than eighty percent of my clients go through these templates in their first coaching season with me. These form the groundwork in setting and achieving any coaching goal or facing any coaching challenge.

Here you'll learn and go through the processes of:

- Goal setting
- Action planning
- Implementing your plan
- Solving problems and overcoming obstacles that will be in your path
- Ensuring you sustain your change and re-prioritize your life for greater effectiveness, and
- How to give and receive feedback using the single most powerful coaching tool I have ever come across. One that you can use for yourself, in your job, with your kids—and get the outcomes you want.

First though, we'll look at developing the relationship with your coach (even developing your relationship and effectiveness as your own coach).

Developing the Relationship

"The reality of the other person is not what he reveals to you, but in what he cannot reveal to you. Therefore, if you would understand him, listen not to what he has to say but rather what he does not say."
Khalil Gibran

Sometimes coaching relationships develop naturally and quickly. From the beginning, there is 'chemistry' between the two. You think alike, have similar perspectives and quickly develop mutual trust. More often, these relationships develop over time and your partnership must be cultivated.

It is considered, by most coaches, that the responsibility for making the relationship work belongs to the coach. And whilst that may be true, it takes two hands to clap, and you need to play your part too.

Imagine that you are stressed out, overworked, overly pressured and don't get the recognition you deserve. This may be so close to reality that you won't find it hard to imagine! You want to grow in your career, but are trapped by your current lifestyle and there's a genuine fear that you may be close to burning out. One day, a friend mentions that she has been helped by a coach and suggests that you do the same. At first, you resist. You've seen the hundreds of articles and adverts promising a silver bullet solution to organise your life, reach your dreams, orchestrate your career and get on top of your life.

You wonder if seeing a coach is an admission of desperation . . . but the opposite is probably true. Coaching is recommended more to people who have real potential for growth and promotion but could use help in reclaiming control of their time, move through transitions with confidence, improve their leadership skills, grow through change, re-examine values or sharpen their working styles.

The more resistant, sceptical and hesitant you are, the harder your coach has to work to build the essential level of trust to be effective. The longer you allow this process to take (by resisting) the longer it will take for your coach to really help you.

It can be daunting for you. But preparing your mindset and being open to the possibility that your chosen coach can help you goes a long way to allowing them to start the real work. That's what this filed-guide is all about.

Your first meeting with your coach (or prospective coach) is crucial: it is about getting to know each other, seeing whether the chemistry works, finding commonalities and establishing the ground rules by going through the coaching agreement.

Typical agenda for the first meeting

- Introductions (background, experience, common interests)
- Ground rules (what is acceptable and what is not)
- Objectives (for the meeting and for the relationship)
- Review of the your current situation and personal SWOT analysis

- Discussion on learning/coaching styles
- When, where and how often to meet
- Actions (things to be done before the next meeting)
- Date of next meeting

If the first meeting works, then you will continue to meet, being mindful and respectful of what was agreed. Having a structure to follow for the meetings help you with preparation, for building confidence in each other and for having a productive relationship.

Getting to know you

In your fist meeting with your coach, you can expect your coach to ask you variations of some or all of the following questions:

- Tell me about yourself
- What is going on in your life?
- What would you like to be different?
- What would you like us to talk about?

You can find a fairly typical "Getting to know you" pre-engagement profile or personal information form:

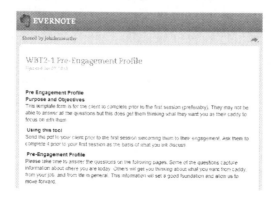

Pre-Engagement Profile http://gainmore.net/wbt-pre

Defining Expectations

A number of coachees overlook this important aspect of the coaching agreement. Defining expectations and monitoring them on a regular basis is important so as to avoid disappointment and to strengthen the relationship.

Your responsibility as the coachee

- To be challenged and stretched, to think more deeply and perhaps learn to be more ambitious
- To respect appointments and the coaching agreement
- To follow through with actions (homework)
- A degree of friendship as your coach needs to feel comfortable with you.
- To be prepared for the coaching relationship
- To challenge the coach in a constructive manner so as to build a mutually beneficial and interesting relationship
- To use coach's time wisely
- To give constructive feedback on the quality of the relationship and on the effectiveness of the feedback

Process of Goal Setting

"A successful process generally begins with setting a well-defined and specific objective, so that you know exactly what you are aiming for and how it appears on the physical level" Yaron Golan

Some of the clients we work with can state their end goal or final objective within the first few minutes of coaching. If you are seeking a new position, learning how to manage your team members or wanting to improve your presentation skills, the coaching may be focused and short-term. More frequently, coaching is broader, often set within the context of your entire life.

Coaching starts with an agreement that something needs to be changed. Then you need to go through a goal-setting process that identifies your own strengths and weaknesses, the opportunities that you might pursue in achieving your goal(s) and the threats or obstacles you are likely to encounter or wish to avoid. It is also well worth your while to examine the external environment, both the macro environment that may affect you indirectly, and the context you are in now and likely to be in for the foreseeable future. This external review will consider the organisational environment, and the people with whom you have relationships, it may include global environmental factors that may have an impact.

If your goal is long-term or broad, you will want to break this down into sub-goals. These will serve as more focused outcomes on the way to achieving your larger goal. Being specific and using the SWING template.

In all of this process, remember that goals are not engraved in stone. They are always open for modification and review. Sometimes, we don't see the whole picture at the beginning and the sub-goals first in a sequence will be clearer than the later ones. As you make progress, any goal can be revised, skipped entirely or abandoned. The intention is to come up with a plan moving forward.

BHAGs

Many people have goals, or at least an idea of what they want to achieve. Usually these are safe, near-sighted, not very challenging and well within your comfort zone. Such goals do little to move you and your life forward. In contrast, BHAGs (Big Hairy Audacious Goals) seem impractical and impossible at first. They stretch everybody. BHAGs are a real push and they force you out of your comfort zone where you can begin to realise something far more than you previously dreamed.

Stretching goals

Leadership and business coaches, like athletic coaches, are often particularly helpful at this stage. Stretching and pushing yourself may not come naturally to you. A coach can help you by nudging you from your familiar and comfortable routines where you typically do the same things in the same way while expecting different results. Stretching is about asking you to become uninhibited, creative and imaginative ways and coming up with new options.

Some times, it may help if you answer the following questions:

- Imagine yourself in the future. How did you get there?
- If money or time were not limited, what would you do now to move forward?
- What might change around you in the future that you need to prepare for now?
- Be creative and consider the resources you could draw on to help you move ahead.

Sensory

When you work through SMARTening up your goals, I ask you to describe your goal in the five senses. I appreciate that many people struggle with the gustatory (smell and taste) though remember that perfume manufacturers spend a vast fortune on developing scent and it is very likely that you use one of them . . . because the smell is evocative and probably reminds you of something dear to you.

When you describe your goal using the five senses (or as many as you can) you are preparing your goal for some means of measurement and have a vision of your goal. Both are powerful ingredients in motivating you (and others) to achieving your goal.

Personal SWOT

"I am always doing that which I can not do, in order that I may learn how to do it." Pablo Picasso

Understand yourself and discover who you are and what you want

You have a choice to make when embarking on any journey. It is possible to simply set off and go somewhere that is anywhere but here. Choose a direction and move! Where do you end up? Well . . . somewhere! This is actually how most people approach their life and their career.

Think about the last time that you decided to go somewhere specific. Firstly you would know where you are at the start of the journey. Then you identify your destination. Then you identify the route from here to there and the means of transport. In choosing the mode of getting from here to there, you would take into consideration what you have that will enable you to get there from here. Perhaps a car, with fuel and of course, you would have the ability and license to drive. If that isn't an option for you, you might choose a bus, a train, maybe even cycle or walk. You would choose the most appropriate transport for you in your circumstances.

The same is true for developing your leadership. Step 1 is to know where you are now.

This is worthy of some serious personal reflection. What are your **strengths** and **weaknesses**? You may have taken our GAPPS Leadership assessment? This is a clear, holistic and objective assessment of your leadership strengths and development needs and an easy place to start this exercise. If you haven't done this yet, you'll need a bit more deep soul-searching. Even with the GAPPS report in hand, you may need to dig deeper.

In addition to this, identify the **opportunities** and **threats** to yourself and your leadership future.

You will map your Strengths, Weaknesses, Opportunities and Threats on a grid. (Yes, it's the same idea as an organization SWOT analysis).

Together, your strengths and opportunities help identify your long-term goals. While your weaknesses and the threats facing you need to be mitigated, planned for or managed to ensure that your goals remain attainable and realistic.

To begin your personal SWOT analysis, you begin by asking yourself a series of questions, answering them in the appropriate of each of the four quadrants:

Personal SWOT Analysis

Strengths

What sets you apart from others?

Your GAPPS report will have identified your leadership strengths and you should include these here.

Think also about your other strengths, all of your experience, education, hobbies as well.

- What are you really good at?
- What do other people ask you to do for them?
- What have you done that makes you really proud
- What connections do you have access to that others do not have?
- What skills do others recognise in you?

Do ask your family, friends and colleagues for honest and candid feedback here. If they suggest something is weak, when you believe it a strength, thank them for their honesty and put it in the next column. (Maybe they are wrong, but it is how they perceive and what they see is often more real than our reflection—think of photos of you.)

Weaknesses

The trick here is to be utterly honest with yourself. Accept that you do have weaker areas, especially if you thought that you were good here but after asking your friends or colleagues, they said otherwise, well those belong here.

These things are to be reduced or managed.

Be fair to yourself, and forgiving (just as you are with others' weaknesses).

- What tasks do you do only because you have to do them?
- When are you most vulnerable?
- Where do you lack resources, connections or experience where others have them?
- In which tasks do you struggle to master?
- Is there anything about your personality or character that holds you back?

Opportunities

Now turn attention to what's happening outside that may be leveraged to your advantage. The economy is often mentioned here or under threats.

- What are the opportunities for someone who does X well? (where X is a specific skills, knowledge or resource)
- Given a fair world and the chance, what would you do that you would truly love and enjoy?
- What would you advise someone possessing your strengths that they could do?
- What trends do you see or have heard about, that have an impact on your career?
- Where is the easiest growth for you in your career?

Threats

Lastly, consider those things or people who could derail your plans.

Clear consideration of these now will enable you to plan around things that are truly uncontrollable.

- Do you have weaknesses now that are genuinely holding you back.
- What setbacks might you encounter?
- What obstacles have others faced when doing something similar to your plans?
- Is there a person, or people, who are genuinely an obstacle in your plans? (You may be thinking that this particular person is against you and is deliberately blocking your progress. We are not looking to resolve this here, nor is this a time to blame someone else, just note it and later you will plan around the threats.

SWOT template http://gainmore.net/wbt-swot

What about PESTs?

Personal PEST analysis

PEST analysis is another tool commonly used in viewing an organizations environment. It is just as powerful when used for your personal development.

Think of yourself, your skills, knowledge and attributes as a marketable product. Especially critical when you are considering your future career and the options open to you. How do you market yourself internally and externally?

PEST stands for the Political, Economic, Social and Technological factors that affect you and your career. Use the questions to help prompt your analysis and consider all others relevant to you in your context.

Consider the opportunities and threats that you have identified in your SWOT (you will likely think of more as you undertake this exercise).

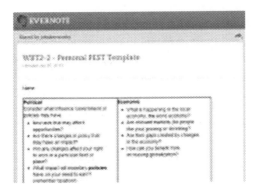

PEST Template http://gainmore.net/wbt-pest

Why set goals?

"A successful process generally begins with setting a well-defined and specific objective, so that you know exactly what you are aiming for and how it appears on the physical level." Yaron Golan

What is a goal?

Hold on just a moment, what do we mean by a 'goal'? Everyone at some point in their life has heard that it is important for us to have goals. Goals provide you a map to your future, whether in business, life, career or indeed sport. It seems obvious, but a football team playing without a goal to aim for is just kicking a ball around. But, other than the more obvious physical goals as the target of a particular game, what exactly is a goal? And how do you know when you have achieved it? Is it even very important to have goals? A sporting goal is a useful analogy though, here we are more interested in the non-sporting variety.

The OED definition of a goal is *"an aim or a desired result"*. That's useful, but I prefer the Wikipedia version which defines a goal as *"a specific, intended result of strategy."* They amount, ultimately to the same thing: the intended achievement of a desired result. The dictionary definition, however, suggests that the goal exists with or without you. Why is this important? I hear some question already. Let me share an example:

On the horizon is a mountain, its peak visible on this glorious day. It is your goal. You are aiming to reach the peak of this mountain.

According to the dictionary the goal is the mountain peak. According to the encyclopaedia, the intended result is that you reach the mountain peak as a result of the journey (intended strategy) you are making.

What's important, the existence of the goal or the journey to its attainment?

Let me refer briefly back to soccer . . . Is the existence of the goal at the end of the pitch the thing that makes the game, or is it the strategy (and tactics) employed by players to score (reach) the goal?

The reason for being pedantic at this stage is to stress that we refer (in English) to goal as both an entity and as the intended result of our actions. For the purposes of this tutorial, I refer to goal as both—an entity that we are able to describe in one or more of the five senses we enjoy and as a specific, intended result. I believe that it is critical that a goal can be described in one or more of our senses—otherwise we will never know what it is.

> *"A man without a goal, you are like a ship without a rudder." Thomas Carlyle*

You know people, perhaps yourself, who would be lost without a "To Do" list. Daily, weekly, monthly tasks that result in specific intended results. Many people will consider this as their goal. Indeed, you can call them 'goals' if you wish. But I want to distinguish this concept further. I call these daily, weekly, monthly tasks "Outcomes"—they are important steps on the way to achieving goals but they are a small part of the overall intended result.

I'll borrow from my own To Do list for today. It includes, strangely enough, writing the first three sections of this tutorial. Now, is my goal to write three sections of a tutorial? Is it to write a tutorial? I can answer yes to both yet it doesn't tell us the full story—my Goal is to develop my business and as a part of that, I want to reach a wider audience for the purpose of building my brand, building my reputation and establishing myself as a trusted expert that you will now consider to undertake coaching with you or within your organisation. This tutorial is just one part of that strategy, and this section, just one part of this tutorial. The primary and secondary research I've undertaken to be in a position to write, I trust, knowledgeably about goal-setting has been another part . . . and so on.

It is the goal that helps us determine the appropriate outcomes necessary to reach the goal, the specific outcomes help determine the actions we undertake to achieve them. The whole series together, makes a strategy.

For ease and clarity, I consider a "Goal" to be longer-term and the intended result of a strategy. "Outcomes" are the result of the steps, milestones or activities that we achieve en-route to achieving the goal.

When I was a child, schoolteachers and relatives would often ask "And what do you want to be when you grow up?" I honestly didn't have a clue. My friends seemed to have got the hand of this and I discovered that the expected answers seemed to be focusing around jobs or careers "I want to be a Fireman/Doctor/ Train Driver", or perhaps something bolder like "Rock Star/Famous Actor"—or around money . . . "I want to be a millionaire". Apparently it didn't matter what you wanted to be—it still required that you studied hard, preferably got all A Grades—oh and it was critically important that you "eat all your greens". Quite how Brussels Sprouts are a necessity for success has never been answered fully to my satisfaction. By the time I was a teenager, I was at the "I dunno" stage. And by the time I was choosing my A level subjects it seemed that my options were becoming limited. Artist was ruled out on the recommendation of my delightful art teacher who claimed that my lovingly crafted painting "hurt her eyes" and Author was ruled out because I had little taste for over-analysing Jane Austin's Northanger Abbey.

To my knowledge, none of my friends answered "I wish to be a wage slave pushing paper from one side of a building to another, politically manoeuvring myself into a position of power and authority, attending useless meetings each day and commute for 4 hours" so what went wrong?

Well, perhaps it is the goal-setting process.

What is goal setting?

Inadvertently, or deliberately, people asking us when young "what do you want to be . . ." have set us on a process of goal-setting. They are asking us to peer in our mind's eye into the distant future and describe our goal. With little worldly experience, we most likely think of people we admire that through their job demonstrate what is valuable to our young minds.

Goal-setting is a process by which we choose our intended result, decide what we want to achieve in the longer-term AND determine HOW we are going to attain the goal (i.e., the strategy). Therein lies the problem for many people in regard to goal-setting . . . the process necessarily includes the strategy to achieve the goal. When relatives with kind intentions ask "what do you want to be . . ." the strategy they advise to achieve whatever you said, invariably refers back to the need to study hard, be a good child, don't answer back and above all . . . "eat your greens!" As you get older, the advice may become more specific and even, more useful. You begin to discover which areas of knowledge and skill you most enjoy and are better equipped to clarify your personal goal as you become increasingly aware of what is important to you.

Goal-setting for your career, life and business is strongly advocated and endorsed in hundreds of books and papers and articles. Most emphasise the importance of writing your goals down as part of the goal-setting process.

Is goal-setting important?

Ask almost anyone about the importance of goal-setting and they will affirm that it is incredibly important. Here is a small selection of verbatim responses to the question "How important is goal-setting?"

> *"The difference between successful people [and people struggling] is the setting of tangible and measurable goals." "I believe goal setting does work and needs to be written down." "If there are no set goals, things either happen, or they don't." "With measurable goals you are in action to fulfil them" ". . . there's no excuse for failing to progress if you don't take ownership of your own goals" "Setting*

yourself some goals is always going to be effective"
"I have been setting goals for myself for over 10
years. I believe that the goals enable me to achieve
the things that I want" "People who are successful
tend to be the same sort that write down goals"

Why set goals?

Edwin Lock and Gary Latham have undertaken a great deal of leading research about goals and goal-setting and neatly suggest that setting goals implies dissatisfaction with the current condition and a desire to attain an outcome[1].

Why Specific and Stretching?

In Locke and Latham's 2006 study and previous articles, there is an emphasis on the positive relationship between goal difficulty and performance[23]. That is, the more difficult the goal is to achieve, **the higher the level of performance is manifest**—albeit moderated by commitment to the goal. Earlier studies had already identified that specific and difficult goals led to greater performance than easy and/ or vague goals[4].

[1]   Locke, Edwin A. and Gary P. Latham (2006), 'New directions in goal-setting theory', Current Directions in Psychological Science, 15 (5), 265-68.

[2]   Locke, Edwin A. and Gary P. Latham (1990), A theory of goal setting and task performance, (Englewood Cliffs, NJ: Prentice-Hall).

[3]   Locke, Edwin A. and G.P. Latham (2002), 'Building a practically useful theory of goal-setting and task motivation', American Psychologist, 57 (9), 705-17

[4]   Loche, Edwin P. (ed.) (1986), Goal setting, Generalizating from Laboratory to Field Settings, Lexington, MA: Lexington Books) 101-17.

Commitment to achieving a goal—Attainable and Realistic

Hollenbeck and Klein, 1987[5] suggest that an individual's commitment to a goal (building on Locke's research and many others) is dependent on a combination of the expectancy that the individual has of achieving success, and the difficulty of achieving the goal. In the commonly used mnemonic, SMART goals, this is usually considered as the 'AR' of SMART—Attainable and Realistic. Though Hollenbeck and Klein help point out that when we set a goal, it may well seem that the goal is attainable—I can do everything that I need to do to achieve this and am prepared for the cost in time, effort, etc.—and it may well seem to be realistic—Given the resources that I have and the current environment, this goal can be practically achieved.

Measurable and Time-bound?

I don't think it would be possible to undertake research on something that had no measure nor a time restriction—how would you know that you had achieved success if there was no measure, and if there is no time limit, when would you stop measuring or even not measuring. So these remain 'common sense' though a post-modernist might disagree.

Does that mean it is true for everyone? To help answer this, we undertook primary research to mirror the mythical Yale Study. Through a simple questionnaire, respondents were asked if they had set goals for themself on leaving school, college or university, when this was and if they had written it down. They were then asked to estimate their total personal wealth now. The results are quite shocking.

---

[5]   Hollenbeck, John R. and Howard Klein, J. (1987), 'Goal Commitment and the Goal-Setting Process: Problems, Prospects, and Proposals for Future Research', Journal of Applied Psychology, 72 (2), 212-20.

There is some strong support for the concept of SMART goals. Goals that are Specific and Stretching, Measurable, Attainable, Realistic and Time-bound. There's a great deal of common sense reasoning that supports the idea of SMART goals—and there's some excellent robust research.

Results from our survey

215 individuals completed the online questionnaire over a seven week period in 2007. Respondents were mostly UK-based (80%), with further respondents from Asia (11%) and the USA (9%). This researcher invited respondents through social networks, Ecademy and LinkedIn and direct contact with companies across the UK, Asia and US. 70% of respondents are in full-time employment, and the remainder either self-employed or business owners.

Only results shown to be significant at 0.05 are discussed.

- At the end of their formal education, 69.8% had a personal goal of whom only 11.2% had written their goal down.

Goals and personal wealth

- Of those that had written their goal, their average personal wealth is GBP115000, whereas those who had not written their goal down, their average personal wealth was GBP295000. That's more than two and a half times as much! Completely contrary to the supposed Yale Study.

We asked respondents when they left formal education and analysed this against their estimated personal wealth.

- Those leaving formal education in the 1970's have an average wealth of GBP475000, 80's GBP195000 and 90's . . . GBP325000!

It seems reasonable that those who have been in the workforce longer would have greater personal wealth and so it is . . . almost. The anomaly appears to be those who left formal education during the 80's.

- Those leaving in the 70's have generated on average 13,500 each year since leaving. 80's grads a miserly 7,800 and those bright young things from the 90's, a whopping 21,600!

So what's going on?

It may have something to do with SMART goals.

SMART goals and personal wealth

- Those who set Specific Measurable only goals average a low 25,000
- Add Time-bound to specific and measurable and this goes up to 50,000
- Just Attainable and Realistic goals—now this is averaging 150,000
- Specific, Measurable, realistic and time-bound and we rise rapidly to 475,000
- Go the whole hog, Specific, measurable, Attainable, Realistic and Time-bound—and we reach 605,000

We seem to be finding some useful answers here. Don't worry so much about writing your goals down, just so long as they're

SMART. So is that it? No. There's a couple of very interesting additional significant statistics in our survey. They deal with the type of goal.

Goal focus and personal wealth

Respondents were asked if they were willing to share their own personal goal, 60% did so and these break down into four main focuses: Career, Lifestyle, Money or Ability. We also asked how satisfied respondents were with their achievement.

For those with a Lifestyle goal focus, average wealth is 95,000 and 'satisfied' with their achievement.

A Career focus, average wealth is just over 100,000 and 'somewhat satisfied'

A Money focus, average wealth is 162,500 and 'satisfied' and lastly,

An 'Ability' focus, average wealth is 780,000 and 'very satisfied'!

Go on, have a guess on the statistical conclusion . . . yep, those who left formal education in the 90's focus more on 'Ability', 80's focus on career and lifestyle, whilst the 70's predominantly Money. Surely a reflection of the environment of the time.

The great thing about focusing on what you are 'able' to do will help the goal-setting process be more effective. Following Locke and Latham's findings that ability to achieve the goal moderates performance—too difficult and uncommitted individuals do not perform, whereas, stretching yet within my potential ability aids commitment to goal attainment

Outcome goals—some issues

The problem facing many people with regard to 'Outcome' goals is that there is an element that is outside the power of the individual. An example of the potential issues with an 'outcome' goal comes from a rather sad testimony from one particular research participant:

> *"My goal was to have $3 million in the bank for my retirement by age 55. I achieved my goal with great satisfaction early at age 43. Unfortunately my bank was at the centre of a fraud and went under. 16 years later, I am still working and slowly rebuilding my goal. So, goals are important and we need to know what we want to achieve in life—just choose a goal only including yourself and don't leave all of it in one place."*

Outcome goals are most often subject to others and to the environment. The greater the attainability of a goal through yourself only—i.e. Your own performance—the more you are in control of goal achievement. Goals that have a high dependence on others and/or external circumstances are considerably more difficult to influence.

As an extreme example, one survey participant has goal to win the lottery! Now there are certain things that you can do to increase the likelihood of this becoming reality, buying tickets is a useful component, but how many? Interestingly, another participant who had a 'money' goal did indeed achieve their goal—through winning the lottery! Though that wasn't the original plan and they rated themselves 'somewhat satisfied' in having completely achieved their goal.

Whilst touching on monetary goals, another participant reminds us that being specific about your goal is important: "My goal was to be a millionaire by 35 . . . I achieved it the moment I stepped away from the foreign exchange counter at Jakarta airport!"

Following up with our survey participants revealed commonality in the way they went about setting goals and their subsequent actions to achieve their goals. We've already seen how those with the greatest success in terms of personal wealth had SMART goals. This isn't to say that success can only be measured by means of personal wealth at all. And, of course, someone could have set themselves a perfectly good SMART goal—but due to their own environment, had not accumulated as much personal wealth in terms of a standard currency—indeed, a person could have less in terms of monetary wealth yet be considerably better off in terms of the value they can obtain from less money.

Performance goals

An interesting aspect that began to show itself through the results was personal satisfaction in goal achievement. People who set 'Ability' type goals, or 'Performance' goals reported to be 'very satisfied' with their achievements—whether completely achieved goals or not yet complete. In part, this suggests the importance of personal values and suggests a question about the process by which they set goals.

Through a random selection of fifty respondents we found that there is some commonality in the manner in which goals are set:

- When we compare the groups of 'Very Satisfied' with their achievement and 'Satisfied' or 'Somewhat Satisfied' with their achievement. The first group was more likely to have SMART goals. The goal is described in sensory terms—what will be seen, heard and felt, and for a small number, smelt and tasted. Respondents were clear about what achieving the goal will do positively for them and the cost to themselves (and others) of achieving their goal. Their goal, they considered personally stretching yet 'knew' that they were capable of achieving it themselves. More than 60% stated their goal in the present tense—'I am' rather than 'I will be'.

This provides a template for a useful goal-setting process that we've turned into an easy-to-remember acronym: SWING.

Goal setting process

A **S**MART and Sensory performance goal **W**hat will I positively **W**in and lose Am **I** In control of achieving this goal? Stated as **N**ow **G**uarantee—this is an added psychological process to ensure personal motivation towards achieving the goal.

Final thoughts

From our survey, those individuals who set performance goals using slight variations of this process represent a small, though statistically significant fraction of the sample that have a net higher annualised personal wealth accumulation (2.15 times) and are more satisfied than individuals who use only one or two aspects of this process.

A SMART goal with an emphasis on performance or ability and the process of thinking through the goal. And for those of you, like me, who just didn't get round to setting goals way back and worry that you might have missed out—well you can't go back and revise history, but you can create a new one now.

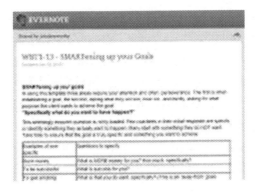

SMARTening up my goals template http://gainmore.net/wbt-smart

SMARTening up your goals

"In preparing for battle I have always found that plans are useless, but planning is indispensable."
Dwight David Eisenhower

Setting Goals

Have you ever set out from your home on a "coin toss tour"? You know, when you decide that you're leaving home and then going left, right or straight on is determined by a coin toss. No? You have no idea where you would end up or when would you?

How about driving somewhere you have never been, without a map? Sure you have some vague idea it's north, but which route is best? Did you miss the turning? Did you refuse stubbornly to ask anyone for directions? Oh . . . a few nods there.

So, pray tell, why do so many people do this with their life and career?

- The first leaves everything to 'chance', to 'fate'. Perhaps it will be exciting and it is an adventure or maybe it will be a dead-end street in the back alley of the rough end of town where nobody walks alone at night . . .
- The second 'feels' right or not . . . and after all you do have a vague idea of where you are going . . . where are you right now though?

How about giving a friend directions to their new home when you have no idea where their new home is? No? Why not?

Wouldn't you want to know the address and then, perhaps you know how to get there already or you can find a suitable map. Then you'll want to know where they are now and then plan a route for them. Then you could give them route markers to watch out for, road names, landmarks . . . milestones.

We've already understood that coaching is about change. You probably already know what you do not want and you may know what you want to do differently—so you know you want to leave home and go somewhere else. Where are you going and how are you going to get there?

I can't help you effectively get there as your coach if you don't know where you want to go (and where you are now). Remember a coach is a vehicle to get you from where you are to where you want to be.

It behooves you to know where you want to go. A coach can help you think this through (in fact 80% of my clients do this in their first couple of sessions with me), but you can do a lot of this yourself.

It is possible that you want help from a coach just for this. And that's great. Gaining clarity of purpose is a big area where coaching can help greatly.

SMARTening up your goals

SMARTening up my goals template
http://gainmore.net/wbt smart

SWING outcome setting

"It don't mean a thing if it ain't got that swing".
Duke Ellington

SWING outcome setting

If your SMART goal is quite large or demanding, I recommend that you break it down into smaller outcomes.

Getting quick wins is often key to sustained success. You might use this now if your SMART goal is suitable, or you might return to this after you have put together your action plan and identified several smaller outcomes that will together achieve your SMART goal.

The SWING Outcome template is one of the most important templates I use as a Professional Leadership Caddy. Its principle use is to establish the specific outcomes desired by a client through your coaching and mentoring. Of course, you may be using this several times throughout the engagement.

The template is also powerfully used for Goal Setting—usually longer term goals that indicate what specific outcomes, behaviour changes or mindset shifts that the client will need through your engagement with them.

The last section of the SWING template guarantees motivation to change.

Using this tool

Start the process with this question:

If there was one thing, that if you were to change it, would have the greatest impact on your performance, what would it be?

Specific outcome. Establish this as a specific outcome that is measurable (by the five senses) and is something to move towards achieving. Choosing an outcome that is something to not do in the future needs to be re-framed, for example, "what do you want instead . . . ?" Establish a clearly defined, sensory outcome and check for congruence.

What will I win? There must be pay-offs or benefits to achieving the outcome for you. What are they?

What will it cost? Every outcome demands some payment, occasionally, this will cost money, and it will always cost time, effort, willpower, strength and commitment. Often you can uncover another behavioural change that is necessary before this one is viable (such as "discipline?).

In Control? This establishes what the individual personally controls, and who or what else the individual needs to either control, or gain support.

For example, I am able to control my temper (it is my reaction), but I am not in control of the circumstances (or people) that may trigger my temper reaction. Many people need the empathy and support of those closest to them. Any significant behavioural change, do advise clients that partners may be involved and should be informed.

Now. "Step into the future, having achieved your outcome, please tell me, what you have now achieved?" Prompt yourself that this includes noticing all the sensory results identified above. Some people struggle with this, so try starting your sentence: "I am now . . .".

Guarantee. This is a powerful series of Cartesian logic questions that force an unconscious response and ensure ecology and congruence.

Please do not try to make sense out of these questions. Just ask yourself and respond. If you struggle to respond, just repeat the question. Note down whatever comes to mind when you read the question. The response itself is not relevant here; the enforced unconscious processing is the intent.

SWING outcome setting http://gainmore.net/wbt-swing

Part Two—Learn and Grow

Process of action planning

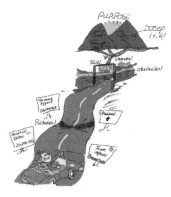

We know from years of experience that setting goals and especially BHAGs (Big Hairy Audacious Goals) is stimulating. When converted into a rich sensory vision, these become incredibly motivating and stimulating, but to make progress we must stop talking and start taking action.

This is where far too many people fail. You probably have some experience of this with new year's resolutions. It's where CEO's fail in leading their organisations to achieve the corporate goals. Political leaders are especially prone to this failure to actually act on their promised vision . . . oh and they can come up with some of the most wonderful excuses and there is always someone else to blame. You too can inspire yourself with great rhetoric and end up not taking action.

Here we can learn much from the best athletic and sports coaches. Teams that win championships are coached by men and women who can articulate their goals, know every players' strengths and weaknesses, push for improvement, encourage and show everyone how to play strategically. If a coach doesn't inspire confidence and check progress, their players may never take action to better themselves or work to win and, as a result, nothing changes.

First you need a plan of action and then the personal commitment to make everything work. This is easier with a coach than doing it alone, though with some self-discipline, you can do it. If you are struggling in actually putting your plan into action, then find a coach or enlist a buddy. Buddying up with someone on the same or similar path is a huge help. Strangely, humans are excellent at letting themselves down but find it much more difficult to let others down (presumably excluding politicians).

Create your Personal Growth Plan

You are now ready to bring all of these pieces together to create your plan. When done, you will have a comprehensive and measurable action plan to monitor your progress and fulfil your dreams.

If you have not taken our GAPPS4 assessment you will need to undertake a skills audit now to ensure that you know what you are good at currently and the areas that you need to develop. If you have taken our full GAPPS4 assessment, use the findings from this to identify your skill strengths and gaps. If you have a report and you want to use a different benchmark (because your career mission has changed) ask your coach for advice.

Remember to add the technical skills and knowledge you will need for your chosen career mission.

Review your SWOT and PEST weaknesses and threats. Do these point to skills that you need to develop to achieve your major career goals? Rate your current ability in each of these skills using a simple scale:

1. High Strength: Skills that I do very well and easily
2. Strength: I can do this and I can improve easily
3. Develop: I need to improve this area

Then against each area, rate each skill area with how important it is for you to achieve your major career goal(s). Use the following scale:

1. Not very critical or important
2. Important
3. Very Important, critical

Then against each skill/ability/knowledge area, identify how easy it is for you to develop in this. Consider such matters as, cost of developing, time to develop, experience needed, access to development (tutors, coach, mentor, boss). Use the following scale:

1. Not easy (e.g. high cost, long time)
2. Reasonably easy
3. Very easy (e.g. I know much of this already or someone to help me)

When you have rated each one, multiply the scores with each other for each ability. The highest score using the scale is 9, the lowest 1.

A 9 is a critical development need that is easy for you to develop and should be a priority—work on these immediately, then deciding between ease of development and how critical that development is for your secondary priorities.

EVERNOTE

Shared by johniesworthy

WBT3-1 - Personal Growth Plan Template

Name:

Area	Specific Behaviour/Ability	a. My Rating	b. Importance to goal	c. Ease of development	Total a x b x c
Applied Business/ Technical Knowledge and skill	Critical Analysis and Judgment				
	Vision and Imagination				
	Strategic Perspective				

Planning for growth http://gainmore.net/wbt-growth

From paper to practice

"Nothing will ever be attempted if all possible objections must first be overcome" Samuel Johnson

Pulling your action plan together

The last step in your planning now is to take the development needs and translate these to specific actions and development that you will do, and by when you will do this. Consider:

- How will I get the training or experience I need (Courses, job-share, on the job training, coaching, training, education)?
- What kind of support do I need? (you know your learning style, do you need someone to nag you? Are you self-disciplined for eLearning?)

- Who will help me? (Enlist the assistance of people who already do this skill well, find a mentor, ask your boss, HR, family, friends)
- How will I reward myself when I achieve this?

Action Plan http://gainmore.net/wbt-plan

Process of implementing

"We are continually faced by great opportunities brilliantly disguised as insoluble problems" Lee Lacocca

Everything till now is entirely possible through self-coaching. This is the part where self-discipline, commitment and follow-through are critical for success in making the changes you want. This is the time when a coach or accountability buddy would be most beneficial.

It's all well and good to have a great SMART goal, several smaller outcomes and a comprehensive action plan. Without the action they just make for great plans and dreams.

Even when you work with a coach, it's still you who has to do the work.

If you are someone who uses to-do lists and actually does what your tasks remind you to do, you may be OK with this step. If not, you can either invest in coaching or (usually somewhat more cheaply) invest in some software that might help you. There are many goal setting systems you could consider that may help or, my personal recommendation, use coachaccountable. No system however, can cause you to actually do what you said you would do.

Perhaps this is the time to let you know that there are no short cuts. There is no 'silver bullet'. No instant success formula. Anyone promising you a 'quick and easy' way to change and have the dreams you desire has an issue with reality and truth.

There are six main areas where a coach can help at this stage of your growth and learning:

1. Giving Feedback
2. Cheerleading
3. Providing accountability
4. Stimulating your self-confidence
5. Empowering
6. Keeping hope alive

Giving Feedback

Feedback is one of the most powerful ways a coach can keep you focused on improving the situation or your performance. In my experience, most people are quick and ready to 'beat themselves up' for doing something wrong or badly. I still do it myself. Rarely do people give themselves positive feedback and, sadly, rarely do we receive positive or reinforcing feedback from others.

This is why I encourage you, nay, implore you to keep a journal and/ or use "What's Better Today?[1] This book was entitled for this and, in my years of coaching and developing others, have found nothing quite as powerful in transforming lives.

---

[1]   http://gainmore.net/wbt-template

Cheerleading

The job of a cheer leader is to encourage the spectators to show their team more support to further encourage the team. So to a coach, at times, will be your cheer leader. Sharing your joy when things go well, and commiserating briefly when things go less well, followed swiftly by more encouragement that you can do it and you can achieve it.

If you don't have someone physically to help you, use the "Who's your Caddy"[2] template again . . . choosing someone who would inspire you as your external viewer.

Providing accountability

It can be difficult to make changes on our own. This is especially true when we are trying to change long-established habits.

Remember with a habit, you get rid of the H, and you still have "a bit". You get rid of the A, and you still have "bit". Then you get rid of the B, and you still have "it". The trick is to get rid of the I, and focus on the "t". Those who have ears to hear . . .

Again, I urge you to keep a journal. (Remember all the great leaders of this world have kept journals . . . otherwise how can they write their memoirs?) Review your journal weekly, monthly and yearly. Share your goals and commitments with someone who cares for you and ask them to help keep you accountable.

Stimulating your self-confidence

Several years ago I stood at the top of an infamous black ski-slope known as "the wall" in Avoriaz, France. It is a long, mogul run

---

[2]   http://gainmore.net/wbt-caddy

very steeply descending from the top of the mountain down to Switzerland below. I was a reasonable skier and had the skills to make it down safely. But standing at the edge, the three or four centimetres before total commitment, my legs were shaking, my heart racing and my fear at an all time high. I was so ready to chicken out and back off. Then my friend came beside me and gently assured me I could do it. Would he come with me? No, but he was going to watch and join me at the bottom by taking the somewhat safer alternate route down on the chair lift. That was all I needed, to know someone thought that I could, even when I feared I could not.

Yes, I did make it. My legs shaking the entire time. I fell once. Just at the restaurant deck as I came to a stop. Exhausted, exhilarated and after a couple of vin chaud with my cheering friend, ready to face it again.

There are times we need re-affirmation of who we are and what we can achieve. People who believe in us and want the best for us. Find someone who will help push you off the edge (in a loving way) and remind you of your own beliefs and principles and to assess the opportunities you have in front of you.

Empowering

To be empowered by someone is to be loaned their power. Sometimes, we need others to do this for us, or to teach us what we need to do. Other times, you can find out how to do something new, or to take a slightly greater risk than you are naturally inclined to take by reading, by watching a movie, a documentary or drawing on your own inner strengths.

There is something in your life that you are talented at doing. It's more than a strength. It's something you are simply very good at doing and probably enjoy doing. It may be a hobby or something you learned when young. If I now asked you how you do it, you'd probably respond: "I don't know, I just do it".

Whatever that talent is (and we all have at least one) reflect on it a moment. At one time, you were unable to do it. But you learned, you persevered, you overcame. Now that you have found that you possess that inner strength, go put it to use in this new area of your life.

Keeping hope alive

A coach can also be someone who helps keep hope alive. Recognise your own efforts and re-affirm your commitment. Things can get better and the change you desire to make will get easier.

Change is uncomfortable. Sit there for a moment with your arms crossed. Now, change the way you cross your arms (instead of left over right, go right over left for example). Comfortable? I thought not. How long or how many times would you have to force yourself to do this before this way of crossing your arms was comfortable? However long or however many, you know that eventually it would be OK. The same is true for the change you want to make. There's hope.

When we move from plan to implementation, a coach will consistently remind you to look for the opportunities to resolve the situation holding fast to your own values and beliefs.

To enable this, you need to be able to assess and analyse the **opportunities** in front of you and to be clear about the **purpose for making the change you want**.

The three templates we will be using are designed to do just this.

Opportunity Analysis

Opportunity Analysis

Having completed your personal SWOT analysis you will have identified particular opportunities. After your PEST analysis, some of these may be especially exciting and others may not be worth pursuing.

- Now is the time to focus on those opportunities that excite you and/or present the best options.
- Talk to people who are already doing this and explore how your strengths stack up to pursuing each option.
- Consider if you have identified a personal weakness that may prove to be an obstacle, and using the PEST analysis, uncover the top 2 or 3 opportunities that represent your preferred choice.

- The more you narrow down the real opportunities, the more enthusiastic effort you can apply to devote to your best choice.

Opportunity analysis template http://gainmore.net/wbt-oa

Values and anchors

"To be authentic means expressing who I am on the inside to the utmost, without calculating the risks involved" Erfat Shani

What are My Values and Anchors

The anchors of our life, and particularly the anchors of our career are informed by our personal values, our perceived competences (job skills) and competencies (leadership skills), our character (the sort of person and leader we are, and our motives).

Knowing ourselves better, by understanding what anchors us, helps in both the decision we make and the direction we take to achieve any goal.

The purpose of this questionnaire is to stimulate your thoughts about your own areas of competence, motives, and values. This questionnaire alone will not reveal your career anchors because it is too easy to bias your answers. However, it will activate your thinking and prepare you for the discussion with your coach.

Values and anchors http://gainmore.net/wbt-values

Rocket ship for life

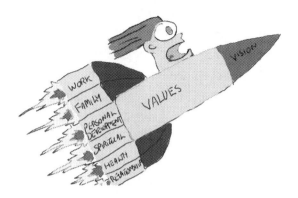

We have different goals in different areas of our lives. In the main, each of us has 6 distinct areas that drive us in our lives. All of our goals are guided by our values, and when we achieve the right balance for ourselves, we can define a clear mission we want to achieve in our lifetime.

It is a little like having a rocket ship for life. The different areas of our lives are the rockets, and the long, medium and short-term goals provide the fuel that drives that area of our life forward. Our guidance system is our personal values. If we have a clear personal mission, we can achieve a purposeful balance—leveraging different goals and energies at appropriate times to move us towards achieving our mission.

There are six goal areas:

1. Work—career, job, employment or business
2. Family

3. Personal Development
4. Relationships (other than family)
5. Spiritual
6. Health

In each area, we have long-term, medium term and short-term goals. What long, medium and short mean for each person may be very different though we do suggest these terms are used in the same context across each area. For example short-term is typically the next 3 to 6 months, medium term, between 6 months and 2 years, long-term more than 2 years.

- It is up to you to define the time frames (which is likely to reflect your current age as well).
- Write down when you will achieve each particular goal. By the way, this particular process goes into personal development under short terms goals.

When you have a few goals noted in each area, ask yourself repeatedly this question: "For what purpose?"

Your 'purpose' suggests personal values.

Combining your goals (usually your longest long-term goals) may be your personal mission—a greater purpose if you like.

Use the template below to help you begin this process. Let the thoughts come to you and keep returning to this to add, alter, adjust or even start over. If this is the first time you have taken time out to reflect on your long-term goals and personal mission, it may take a while to fine tune.

Rocket ship for life http://gainmore.net/wbt-rocket

Overcoming obstacles

*"Courage doesn't always roar. Sometimes courage is
the quiet voice at the end of the day saying 'I will try
again tomorrow.'" Mary Anne Radmacher-Hershey*

If you drive a car, you'll be well acquainted with road construction,
detours, traffic jams and parking tickets. Rarely can someone leave
their home to drive somewhere without some obstacle getting in
the way of a smooth journey. For those of you, like me, who rely
on public transport, the delay of buses, trains and planes is an
everyday occurrence (actually for me that is seldom true since I
live in Singapore but it does happen even here).

The chances are high that you picked up this book because you
were facing an obstacle in your career or life. The equivalent of a
traffic jam or a roadblock. You may have come this far with a clear
vision, SMART goals and a full understanding of the changes you
want to make for purposes that will give you great satisfaction.
Then there's an obstacle.

Real barriers, outside of you, are actually easier to deal with than the internal ones we create for ourselves. Internal obstacles include the more subtle fears, attitudes, insecurities, distractions and habits. An obstacle can make their appearance at any time in coaching and development. Some are common and easily identified. Others are unique and so well disguised that they don't appear until later in the coaching process.

The following list shows the top nine obstacles preventing people from doing what they had agreed to do:

1. I don't know what is expected of me specifically.
2. I don't know how to do it.
3. I don't know why I should do it.
4. I think I am doing it but I'm not getting any feedback.
5. There are obstacles in my way, beyond my control.
6. I don't think it will work.
7. I think my way is better.
8. Something else is more important so I'm doing that now.
9. There is no benefit if I do it.

Do you notice that only one of these top nine 'reasons' is outside of the person's control?

For most people, the obstacles fall into two broad categories:

1. Lack of clarity of direction (goal and specifically what to do)
2. Lack of feedback (unable to evaluate how they are progressing)

External obstacles

There's one thing I can be sure of in your coaching and development, there will be an external obstacle at some time.

Do you have too much to do? Of course you do, so do I. We complain about our hectic lifestyles and too often, busyness is a badge of honour and thought of as a sign of importance. True, much of this busyness is caused by demands from other people. If you are caring for preschool age children or your boss is demanding, you have little control over your schedule. There is little enough time to keep up with the demands of life as it is, let alone work on your own development.

The following list shows some of the common obstacles to development that appear to be rooted in circumstances (or people) beyond our control.

- **Barrier**—impact—*suggestions*
- **Too many demands**—Pressured, distracted by things more urgent—*Re-prioritise, learn to manage time and schedules, find someone to help, delegate.*
- **Difficult people**—Consumes more time, drains energy and enthusiasm, no support or help—*Establish clear boundaries, avoid politiking and power struggles, learn to say "no", confront where you can and re-evaluate your priorities.*
- **Distracting life events**—Consumes energy and diverts attention to the distraction—*Deal with the life event and return to your continued development later.*
- **No accountability**—Lack of motivation and commitment and to keep on keeping on—*Find a buddy to hold you accountable.*
- **Criticism**—Self-doubt, fear of rejection, fear of failure—*Evaluate the criticism, work on valid feedback, don't bother defending yourself or your actions, decide what you will do from now.*

- **No feedback**—Discouraged, confusion, lack of progress—*Find a way to get honest and candid feedback.*
- **Energy vampires**—Interruptions, losing time and patience, distracting—*Identify the energy vampires—if they are people, get them out of your life. If it is something else, find ways to reduce their impact.*

As you look at this list, you will notice that many of these 'external' barriers are actually rooted in ourselves. For example, a demanding schedule is, in my experience, often the result of re-work rather than getting it done right first time. At other times, the demands are high on us because we're not actually very good at doing what is needed . . . you might be surprised how much time you can create for yourself by only working in areas where you have strengths, learning how to delegate effectively to others for your own areas of weakness. Another big problem I find with clients is OOPS or Overly Optimistic Planning Syndrome. A general rule of thumb suggested by successful Project Managers is to take the plan, double the time, double the cost and halve the benefit.

Some of these external obstacles are very real and very difficult to overcome. Distracting life events such as critical illness (of yourself or a loved one), kids needs or a sudden and unexpected loss of income simply consume our time. You have two options: do nothing and give up or determine what you can do to make whatever changes are needed to alter, remove or learn how to live with the barrier.

Common throughout the 'external' obstacles is the energy vampire. Whether the energy vampire is people, pressure of work, or negative emotions like anxiety or depression, or just those thousands of small hassles that, like mosquitoes on a hot and humid day, drive even the calmest person to distraction.

For many, the biggest problem is an overloaded email inbox, or the text message beep that might just be more important than anything else happening right now. I worked with a large organisation soon after the arrival of the Blackberry phone which they had implemented organisation-wide. Senior managers in the company would respond quickly to any and all incoming messages and expected their staff to do the same. After all, wasn't this new technology meant to quicken response? The downside was the very 'macho' culture of being seen to be busy and always in demand led many staff to near nervous breakdown. A beep in the middle of the night could be a client issue across the globe and demanded instant attention. And of course, the off-button simply doesn't work—even weekends and evenings are consumed. Is anybody more productive as a result? It seems the opposite is true.

The elevator principle

Everyone has someone in their lives who, when you see them, they just drain all your energy and enthusiasm for life. They are the energy VAMPIRES. The moment you spot them, you go 'oh crikey, not them, what are they going to take this time?' Duck or run, but if they spot you already . . .

There are some people who lift you up, and others who take you down. Surround yourself with people who raise your energy. These optimistic individuals will encourage you and infect you with enthusiasm. There are some people who light up the room when they walk in, and those who light it up when they walk out. You know the ones you should avoid, you see them coming towards you and immediately you prepare yourself for the bite on the neck as they suck the life blood from you. What to do with them? Get them out of your life. Establish the boundaries and sometimes confront them. If you are a 'people pleaser' and find yourself unable to cut yourself off from them, you're going to have to live with that. It's harsh I know, but you get bitten enough by these energy vampires . . . you can so easily turn into one yourself.

Remember these wise words from Colin Powell—*"When we are debating an issue, loyalty means giving me your honest opinion, whether you think I'll like it or not. Once a decision has been made, the debate ends, loyalty now means executing the decision as if it were your own."*

Internal obstacles

When I first created the GAINMORE Golf Leadership Advantage, a coaching programme on the golf course that equipped and enabled leaders to control their inner thinking, I was astounded with how powerfully leaders began to change for the better. As Tim Galway, author of *The Inner Game of Tennis*, argued that most good players know all about techniques, but many fail to realise that *"the opponent within one's head is more formidable than the one on the other side of the net."*

To thrive in work and life, we must deal with the inner obstacles of resistance to change, procrastination, doubt, boredom and fear of failure. Such thinking undermines our confidence and must be replaced with positive, empowering and goal focused visions and a determined pursuit of our goals.

The following list shows a partial list of the top internal obstacles to development:

- **Barrier**—impact—*suggestions*
- **Fear**—Stops you taking action—*Talk openly and candidly to a friend, challenge self-defeating self-talk, break the change down into smaller outcomes and get quick wins.*

- **Negative mindset**—Believing that it cannot be done—*Catch all negative self-talk and replace with a positive belief in the possible.*
- **Resistance to change**—Lack of cooperation even with up-front agreement—*Review the real value of change for yourself and others.*
- **No ownership**—Motivation to keep on keeping on drops until the project is abandoned—*Choose to be accountable for your own life . . . no-one else cares to do it for you.*
- **Habits**—Get in the way of taking action—*Change the environment or people who encourage the habitual behaviour, admit that habits can be changed by repetition of new behaviours, work with a buddy.*
- **Impatience**—Rushing the process and achieving mediocrity and even failure—*Break the change into smaller outcomes and get quick wins.*
- **Boredom**—Loss of interest and motivation—*Re clarify your goals and link to your passion.*

Internal barriers are mostly emotions that are fed by your thinking or self-talk. It is easier it seems for all humans to dwell on the negative and seemingly much more difficult to mediate on the positive. Your emotions then trigger behaviour and actions.

That is, the process is: Thinking to Emotions to Action.

- So to change an action, we need to change the emotion. To change the emotion we must change the thinking.

Try it. Think of smiling and force yourself (if necessary) to smile. Keep it. Now you feel better.

- If you are feeling tense, just breathe deeply into your belly for 10 long breaths. Count if you like as well.

Why do these work? Well, your thinking brain is essentially slow and lazy and doesn't like doing too much work. So occupying your thinking with 'how to smile . . . which muscles etc' or breathing purposefully' means that your thinking brain cannot also process whatever negative thinking was going on. Added oxygen or the positive physical sensation of a smile then allows your emotional brain to 'believe' that all is well and floods the brain with positive feeling chemicals.

The trick is to catch any and all negative thinking or self-talk . . . fill your thinking with positive thoughts or something that requires effort.

Do this every single time you can catch yourself thinking negative thoughts and it will soon become a habit and to anyone outside, you will appear calm, positive, in control and at peace. In such a space, change is much easier and fears are just a test for you to celebrate overcoming.

We will look at a couple of very useful tools to help you in overcoming obstacles:

1. Understanding the Creative and Survival Cycles, and
2. how to Re-frame Attitudes.

Are you at Cause or Effect?

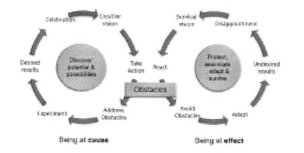

"Life happens whilst you're making other plans."
John Lennon

One of the most common issues faced by people in their lives and leadership is: life happening.

Some of you are going to like this, others won't like this one little bit. Essentially, you have a choice. A very simple choice. You can either choose to create your future, or they can accept the one that you get.

Moving yourself from effect to cause

"But . . ." I hear you about to interrupt . . . there are no 'buts'. Sorry about that. Yes, it is true that other people, the world, the circumstances around you may well prevent you from achieving your goal. So what are you going to **do** about it?

Can you cause the world do something different? There are many things that you cannot change . . . the weather for example. So the answer is . . . . **overcome** the problem.

Can you make another person do whatever is necessary?
Neither I nor you can directly cause them to do something,
though you can influence them.

"But . . ." I continue to hear . . . There are no buts. You **choose** to act to overcome the obstacle.

In any given situation, we start with a choice. We can act to make something happen, or, we react to the external situation. Both appear to start the same way. Yet, they start a cycle that is either virtuous or destructive in the long-term.

Most people who are motivated **towards** achievement and have a "Growth Mindset" are likely to be in the creative cycle. Those of you who are more motivated **away-from** things that you do not want and have a "Fixed Mindset", will be in the survival cycle.

When you are at effect, you **react to something external** to you (or something that you believe is outside your control). Your primary purpose is to protect yourself (or your people).

Your personal values and beliefs will determine what you see as
obstacles, both conscious and unconscious and these influence
your choice to address or avoid the obstacles.

In the **survival cycle**, you will try to avoid the obstacles in your path to reacting to the external 'threat'. And, as you try to avoid them, you will adapt or assimilate your reaction to do so. As a result of obstacle avoidance, your result is likely to be less than optimal. Most often the result achieved is not really the desired result. This leads to disappointment and your survival vision . . . "I have to" . . . "I must . . ." in order to survive.

On the other side, you can choose to take action. The desired end result could be considered to be exactly the same thing, and the external environmental pressures could also be exactly the same as for the person who 'reacts'. It's a mindset choice that makes the greatest difference here. In the **creative cycle**, your purpose is to discover potential and possibilities.

You take action and come across the self-same obstacles. **But instead of trying to avoid the obstacles, you address them**. Experimenting and testing to find the best way to overcome the obstacles. When you find the optimal way to address the obstacle, you gain your desired result and CELEBRATE!. You have a creative vision . . . "I like to . . ." . . . "I want to . . ."

Survival cycle strategies that we employ (and we all employ them at some point) are often developed early in life and were originally a creative response to a situation. It worked then and achieved the desired results then. Later in life, we continue to use the same response yet circumstances have changed.

A common example of taking an early life response and applying it in later life that I come across frequently is when a child's parents use punishment as their primary means of maintaining discipline at home and as their primary means of getting the child to do certain tasks or chores. This often means that you may be choosing to be at cause, and using the creative cycle, yet those obstacles, well they turn out to be insurmountable . . . so you avoid them instead, adapting and assimilating, true, not getting the optimal result but, life really does happen whilst you are making other plans.

Do you want to be at cause for your life, or at the effect of life happening to you?

If you genuinely want the latter . . . read no more, you are in danger of gaining the former.

Are you like a **thermometer**. Reacting to the external environment?

Or, are you like a **thermostat**, changing and adapting and controlling what you can control to change the environment?

In their book "The Skilled Facilitator", Schwarz et al, (2005) they describe a Life Learning Model, developed by Dr. Guillermo Cuellar, adapted in the diagram below to show the creative and survival cycles that people choose to follow.

Some examples of early creative responses that later in life become survival responses:

- Examples of original causes—CREATIVE response when young
  - *Examples of later behaviours in life—that are now SURVIVAL responses*
- "Eat all your dinner or I'll smack you"—'Accidentally' feed the dog under the table (especially those gray Brussels Sprouts!)
  - *Abdicate (aka delegate) work I don't like or enjoy to others. Blame others for the mess they leave. (Think about the many bosses who've dumped their workload on you)*
- "Get a Grade A or I'll beat you"—Hide report cards from parents (get caught eventually but fewer beatings)
  - *Continuously change reporting policies to hide information from stakeholders (think Enron and Kenneth Lay)*

- "Behave or go to your room without supper"—Stock up on foodstuff secretly in room and/or outwardly behave whilst inwardly rebelling. Hardly a punishment if you have Internet and TV in your room but still used.
    - *"Play politics" sucking up to the right people outwardly whilst undermining them to take power away. (Think about Kevin Rudd's sudden resignation as Australia's PM)*

Using the template

This template is a diagram to share consider whilst going through your own issue or obstacle.

- Are you REACTING to something external, or did you choose to take action?
- How are you adapting your behaviour to get around (avoid) the obstacle?
- Can you accept (some or all) of the responsibility for your own actions and behaviours. (That even if this is caused by an external factor, that moaning about that and expecting someone else to deal with it does not resolve the problem for you.)
- Consider the benefits of a creative response
- Most often, you will find new ways to address the obstacle for yourself. Reframing can be used here powerfully.

5 – Creative and Survival Cycle Diagram

This template is a diagram to share consider whilst going through your own issue or obstacle.

* Are you REACTING to something external, or did you choose to take action?
* How are you adapting your behaviour to get around (avoid) the obstacle?
* Can you accept (some or all) of the responsibility for your own actions and behaviours. (That even if this is caused by an external factor, that meaning about that and expecting someone else to deal with it does not resolve the problem for you.)
* Consider the benefits of a creative response
* Most often, you will find new ways to address the obstacle for yourself. Reframing can be used here powerfully.

Click on the image to download a full sized version

Creative and Survival Cycle Diagram http://gainmore.net/wbt-cs

Reframing attitudes

Reframing is a technique to consider an issue as currently seen by deliberately taking a different perspective. Reframing can be broken down into two types—content and context.

Content Reframing

The content of a situation is the meaning that is given to it. The content of what you are saying has a cause and effect structure.

> *Making a mess of that presentation means I am useless at presenting.*

This statement is also a generalisation, because taken in isolation the statement implies that from one single presentation a judgment can be made. When clients make comments like this I have found it helpful to ask questions like:

- According to whom?
- What might be useful about this experience?

- How else could you describe your behaviour in this situation? What can you learn from this experience?
- How would you advise someone who had just given the presentation you did?
- What did you do well?

The whole point is to help you to consider the positive aspects of your own behaviour, to look at the situation from a whole range of different perspectives that may change the way you view the meaning you have given to it.

Context Reframing

The context of a situation or event is about where it occurs. It is a simple fact that any experience, event or behaviour has different implications depending on where it occurs.

You might say:

- 'I spent so much time on the detail that I just didn't get it finished in time
- I'm just too detail conscious!'

This statement focuses on the negative aspect of a particular behaviour but there will be times when being detail conscious serves you well. A useful way of reframing this might be to ask:

- When might being detailed be helpful for you?
- Where could you use this skill in the future?

These questions get you to focus on times when and where attention to detail is important. It can then help you to respond in a more positive way to what you see as a negative behaviour.

This tool works well to:

- Recognise which essential attitude best assists resolving a problem
- Re-define problems by taking a different perspective
- Find solutions to difficult issues

Using this tool

This reframing tool is designed for self-use. You need to be disciplined in your application and make sure that you give yourself new answers. If you are working with a coach, reframing is most often done using questions. I include some common reframing questions as well at the end of this template. First, I recommend using the Five Attitudes Approach.

Reframing using the Five Attitudes Approach

Get six pieces of paper or card and write on them the following:

1. The Problem
2. Respect the OTHER person's model of the world
3. The meaning of your communication is the RESPONSE you get back
4. People are NOT their behaviours
5. People CAN change anything
6. There is NO failure, only feedback
   - Lay the cards on the floor.
   - Choose someone who works with you or with whom you have a difficult relationship. Stand on the "Problem" card.
   - Describe the problem using the following questions:
     - What is the problem?

- What are the consequences of the problem for me?
- What are the implications for others around me?
- How does the problem make me feel? How do I experience that feeling? Can I describe it to me?
- What impact does the problem have on my performance?

• Now, which of the 5 "Attitudes" would best assist in solving this problem?"

• Stand on the most appropriate "Attitude" card and considers the problem from that new attitude.

• Consider the problem ACTING AS IF this attitude were true.

- "Looking at the problem from this attitude what options do you have?"
- "What will the pay-offs be for adopting this new attitude?"

• Now you have a new approach to the problem.

Test the problem with each of the five attitudes, always acting as if this attitude were true. One or more of these attitudes will offer a possible solution.

We have yet to come across a problem that does not change after genuinely reframing the problem using one or more of these five attitudes. Actually, there are exceptions: problems that do not involve people in any way, which isn't many.

Our normal world view tends to view problems as, well, problems. We have our view and often get caught up in the emotion of doing something about the problem (ignoring the problem is still doing something about it).

Take time with each and every problem you come across. Deliberately choose one of these attitudes. I recommend deliberately shifting your body to take a different view. ACT as if the attitude is true. Consider the problem in just the same manner as this exercise.

Reframing using Questions

Whatever your issue or obstacle, ask yourself any (or all!) of these questions:

- Does the problem lie in the task itself, or the way you feel about the task?
- What "rules" do you have for yourself that could be changed?
- What is the positive in this experience?
- If you were already a successful businessman, how would you go about this?
- What would your role model do in this situation?
- What would your coach say about this situation?
- What resources do you have to assist you here?
- What else could this situation mean?
- How can you learn from this?
- What did you learn from this?
- What other ways could you look at this?
- What will this help you accomplish in the future?
- What would your best friend do in this situation?
- What else have I been afraid of but accomplished anyway?
- What is another way to go about this?
- What could you do differently?
- Who would help you with this?
- What is one small thing you could do right now?
- How can I communicate this differently?
- How can a cool company find me to work for them?

- How has this helped you to move closer to your desired outcome?
- If your best friend was in this situation, what would you advise her to do?
- How you make this task/event/situation fun?
- What other direction can you now try?
- So what now?
- I know you do not know, but if you did?

Development and growth

"One's philosophy is not best expressed in words; it is expressed in the choices one makes . . . . In the long run, we shape our lives and we shape ourselves. The process never ends until we die. And the choices we make are ultimately our own responsibility." Eleanor Roosevelt

Everyone wants to improve, but not all want to change. The problem is that if we want to improve, we need to develop and grow, and that requires us to change. Whatever type of improvement or change you want to make, unless you go about growing intentionally, the effect will only be skin-deep and probably won't be sustained.

It's easy for us to get into one of life's ruts. We find ourselves in a comfort zone in some part of our life and continue in the groove even when it's heading in the wrong direction. If we learn something, it's by accident. We just get by and most of the time we remain in survival mode.

In the Survival Cycle with a largely Fixed Mindset, growth happens accidentally. In the Creative Cycle with a largely Growth Mindset, we can choose to be intentional about our growth and development.

You have a choice:

Accidental growth and development

- Talk big
- Plan to start tomorrow
- Wait for growth to come
- Play it safe
- Depend on good luck
- Quit early and often
- Fall into bad habits
- Think like a victim
- Learn only from mistakes

Intentional growth and development

- Think like a learner
- Start today
- Choose to grow
- Rely on hard work
- Keep on keeping on through the tough days too
- Work on good habits
- Think like a victor
- Take risks
- Never stop growing

Growth doesn't just happen—not for me, not for you, not for anybody. You have to go after it and you have to work at it!

With the decision and follow through of intentional growth there are two areas which can derail your new intention:

- Maintaining your motivation and
- Prioritising growth

I have lost count of the number of clients who have told me at the beginning of a session that they had been too busy to do the homework. And all of them have excellent reasons for their time being filled. I shared about these valid reasons in "Overcoming obstacles".

If you do not make the time, no one will make it for you. It's either your drive and motivation for growing and developing (compared to those other things you complain about having to do) or it's the way you prioritise your time.

Motivation to grow

Where are you living?

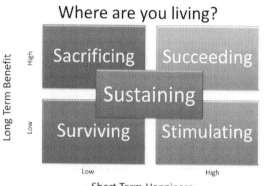

Long Term Benefit — High / Low

Sacrificing	Succeeding
Sustaining	
Surviving	Stimulating

Low — High

Short Term Happiness

Personal Motivations to grow

Some people are totally charged up about what they do and where they are going, whilst others feel that each day is something of a trial and growth and development is a burden. Where are you in this? **Do you love what you do each day?**

For many people their personal strengths, knowledge and expertise may have been programmed into them. They end up in a particular career path, working for a particular type of organisation because, from an early age, other people (parents, teachers, mentors) influenced their choices.

Some people are in a particular career because this is what they studied to do. Sadly, this does not necessarily mean that they enjoy doing it. Of course, every career has some elements that we enjoy less than others but what is the right balance for you?

We can assess our strengths and weaknesses further by rating out of 10 for each activity within a job against two questions:

1. **How much long-term benefit or meaning did I experience from this activity?**
2. **How much short-term happiness or satisfaction did I experience from this activity?**

There are no "right" answers to these questions and your rating score is entirely down to you (by all means keep changing it until you work out what is really a 10, and what is really a 1)

Consider your current job (or whatever you are doing now) and take a typical day (a week if you change what you do each day) and record what you do, for how long and what score out of ten you give that activity against the two questions.

For example, you may spend 3 hours in meetings, 1 hour traveling to and from work, 90 minutes on emails, 30 minutes surfing the net searching for information, 30 minutes in the coffee-room, an hour for lunch, 2 hours preparing a presentation, 30 minutes on phone calls to clients. This might look something like this:

Activity	Time	Long term benefit	Short term happiness
Bible Study	0.5	6	6
Personal development	2	9	7
Travel to work	0.5	1	1
Meetings	3	6	3
Emails	1.5	3	5
Net searching	0.5	2	7

Personal motivations template example
http://gainmore.net/wbt motiv-ex

Remember, this is just an example, you can break it down further and of course, you will have more distinct activities in your day.

The benefit of doing this is that you quickly identify the activities that you enjoy doing the most and those that bring you the most benefit. Searching the Internet for example, can be very satisfactory in the short-term, especially if you are searching for something in your area of interest. But half an hour can disappear with little to show in actual useful long-term results.

In an ideal perfect world, we would find great short-term happiness in everything we do and each reaps long-term benefit. In reality, we all do things that run short of the perfect score for us, but the more we can get the balance and the higher the better. For high performance you do those things that bring the greatest long-term benefit in the shortest time. For most fun you do those things that bring the greatest happiness over the longest period of time. In the end, it's your choice but the better the overall balance the more likely you are to enjoy each and every day.

You can then plot your regular activities on a chart like the one above. Which activities are Surviving, which stimulating, sacrificing succeeding or are they sustaining?

Taking the example above, these activities would be something like this:

Activity	Time	Long term benefit	Short term happiness
Bible Study	0 5	8	6
Personal development	2	9	7
Travel to work	0.5	4	1
Meetings	3	6	3
Emails	1 5	3	5
Net searching	0 5	2	7
Coffee	0 5	1	9
Lunch (with client)	1	7	6
Prepare presentation	2	6	4
Phone calls	0 5	5	4
Travel home	0 5	3	6
Dinner at home with family	1	5	8

- Where is your personal growth and development time?

If you are sacrificing now, then you'll need to be sure that you keep it up and break it down into smaller wins (which will increase short-term happiness). If it's in Succeeding, great. Anywhere else . . . then you are very likely to give up when the hard work kicks in or when there are setbacks. Then you probably need someone else to help you.

And of course, in a perfect world you would get everything you do into the succeeding quadrant. When everything that you do you do so very happily and everything brings a long-term benefit.

EVERNOTE

Shared by johnkenworthy

WBT6-1 - Personal Motivations for growth Template
updated on 07 2015

Name:

Activity	Time	Long term benefit	Short term happiness	Where am I living?
Personal Development and growth				

Personal motivations for growth http://gainmore.net/wbt-motiv

Rule of 5

It's my own fault. I forgot to put breathing on my to-do list

"There are no short cuts to the places that are worth going to" Erfat Shani

Dr John C. Maxwell share this tip about doing anything. It's the rule of 5.

Imagine that you have a tree in your garden that you want to chop down. You find an axe and, after sharpening it, have a go at the tree. But this is a big tree. And your axe is quite small. You can't get another axe, there are none to be had anywhere. So you swing at it repeatedly and the tree remains stubbornly up. Damaged but still very much there.

The rule of 5 tells you that you go to the tree with your axe everyday and take 5 swings at it. Just 5. Put the axe away and return the next day and take 5 more swings at it. Then the next day, the next and so on.

Eventually, that tree is going to come down.

5 swings with the axe is enough to do, it's not too much and it's not too taxing. Just do it every day.

John Maxwell suggests that we should all have 5 things that we do every day.

I started doing this 2 years ago.

1. Everyday I read.
2. Everyday I think.
3. Everyday I write.
4. Everyday I ask questions.
5. Everyday I thank God.

The result is this book, and two others in production, 3 new training programmes and a fulfilled life.

It's not a quick fix. I've tried plenty of those. I've tried to-do lists, several 'time-management' techniques. This one works. It's the easiest form of self-discipline and diligence for me, includes my own constant intentional growth and development (it's what you read, think about and ask questions about). Try it with your own five things. Start with one or two and build up . . . but stick to five things that you do everyday.

- "What do you mean every day?" Every day.
- "What about weekends?" Every day.
- "What about Christmas and holidays?" Every day.

Consistency on a daily basis of doing something that is a goal will give you the desired achievement over time. You don't have to do it all day, but you do have to do it every day.

Prioritisation

"Getting started is breaking your complex overwhelming tasks into small manageable tasks, and then starting on the first one." Mark Twain

Most clients when I ask them, tell me that they prioritise based on urgency trumping importance. This leads to stress and lack of accomplishment. Great leaders know the difference between being busy and accomplishment. It really doesn't matter how busy you are. It's what you achieve that makes a difference. This was one of my big weaknesses. And, if I am not careful, can easily be again. I can easily get distracted by something new and shiny . . . especially some new technology. I am getting better, but it still requires my self-discipline and diligence to keep this up. Again, it was Dr John C. Maxwell who suggests this and I have shared this with many clients as it works well and better than other ways of prioritising or so-called "timemanagement". We start with the Three R's of prioritisation and then use the 80/20 rule. The Three R's of Prioritisation:

1. **Required**—What things must I do that nobody else can or should do for me?

2. **Return**—What gives the greatest return on my time and effort? What am I doing that can be done at least 80% as well by someone else?

3. **Reward**—What things do I enjoy doing, that I am passionate about? Doing the things that you love to do is fuel for your soul and body.

Create a list of things that fit each of these categories. Anything that can or should be done by someone else needs to be, well, done by someone else. And make sure that you keep some things in reward (even if they could or should be done by someone else).

Now we apply the 80/20 rule or Pareto analysis

The idea of Pareto analysis is that 20% of activity produces 80% of the result. It follows pretty well throughout all aspects of life. 20% of the sales people deliver 80% of the sales. 20% of your products deliver 80% of your profit. In the same way 20% of your own effort produces 80% of your results.

So things we have to do (required) are part of the 20%. Intentional growth and development is also part of your 20%. The remaining 80% of your time you should spend doing things that give you the greatest return and things that you find rewarding.

In short:

- Spend 80% of your time in your strength zone—things that you are good at doing (and thus do quickly and easily)
- Spend 15% of your time doing things that are required of you, but you are neither especially strong at doing nor are you so appallingly bad at doing that you really should hire someone to do it.

- Spend 5% of your time intentionally learning, developing and growing.

As for "time-management". You cannot manage time. Time will keep on tick-tocking away whatever you do. But in the wonderful wisdom of John Wooden "Make everyday your masterpiece".

Give 100% today, for tomorrow you cannot make up to more than 100%.

I have taken the same activities as used in the example for personal motivations and applied the rulings here to show you how this can work to re-prioritise the daily activities:

Activity	Required	Return	Reward	Strength 80%	Must Do 15%	Learning and growth 5%
Bible Study			X			X
Personal development		X		X		X
Travel to work	X				X	
Meetings		X		X	X	
Emails		X			X	
Net searching			X			
Coffee						
Lunch (with client)	X			X		
Prepare presentation		X		X		
Phone calls	X				X	
Travel home			X		X	
Dinner at home with family			X	X		

Prioritization template example http://gainmore.net/wbt-prior-ex

Now, it is quick to see which activities should be at the lowest priority. In this example Coffee and net searching. If time is short, these might have to go first.

- And some activities might fit more than one column in time allocation.
- Use your own activities list and then re-prioritise.

"But I have to attend meetings and there's never any point to them, they are just a waste of mine, and everyone's time." You are far from being alone if you have this question or a similar one. So, does the meeting fit 'Required'? (Test this, don't just assume that someone calls a meeting and that you have to attend). Are meetings something you are strong at? (Perhaps you could chair the meeting to make sure it achieves what is intended?) Do you really have to attend? (You need to know when to push back and when to back off leading up if this is your boss.) Is the meeting a learning opportunity?

I'd suggest that you don't expect this to be perfect straight away, but as you move your time spent into your strength zone—you'll find that urgency is rarely an issue and when it is, it is the genuine unforeseen circumstances . . . another opportunity to learn, reflect and grow . . .

Prioritization template http://gainmore.net/wbt-prior

Reviewing

"I shut my eyes in order to see" Paul Gauguin

Acting on feedback is one of the most, if not the most effective means of learning and growing. Yet so few people receive useful feedback.

- How often have you received feedback that clearly identified for you what you did well and specifically what you could do to improve?

When I was at school, I received plenty of less than positive feedback in the form of low marks and poor grades. My school reports were filled with "could do better" or "could try harder" statements. My parents would then ask me what I needed to do better. Well I honestly didn't have a clue. I, of course, knew that I hadn't worked as hard as most of my classmates. I also knew that some of my homework had been a little rushed and lackadaisical.

Even my teachers at the time when I asked about the required outcomes (I wasn't quite this clear of course) and what specifically I needed to do "better" or "harder" gave me short shrift. When I started my career in the kitchens of a hotel, I had a little more clarity about the expectations of my role. However many dirty pots in site were to be cleaned. Floors scrubbed. Potatoes peeled and so on. At least I knew what I was supposed to achieve and could easily see whether I had achieved it or not. But feedback? Sure, I either got shouted at, locked in the walk-in freezer, told to keep working until everything was done or, blessed day . . . got an actual "well done" . . . once!

- When was the last time your boss told you what you had done well and what you could do to improve? I know, rare isn't it? You probably have heard that you need to "do better", "try harder". "do it faster" or similar? But here's the nasty question . . . **when did you last tell your team members what they were doing well and what they needed to improve?** Yes, of course, the annual performance review. When you get a grading of some sort for your performance and all the myriad reasons it isn't as good as you thought it should be. And had you, 11 months previously done something different . . . all would be well . . .
- When was the last time you reviewed your own performance? Prior to reading this book?

I want to share with you the two single most powerful tools you can put to use today that will improve your performance and start improving your staff performance. I'll start with the latter—giving feedback to others—as this will be one thing you can do to develop your team immediately—this will make you a better, more respected and effective leader. Then I'll end this part with my favourite tool and the title of this book—**What's Better Today?**

Feedback sandwich—nourishment for your learning and growth

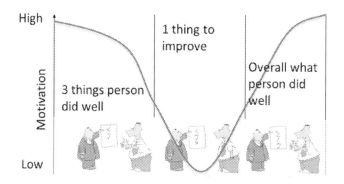

High performance coaching and mentoring is a regular and continuous process. It is something that the leader does every day. *The most effective means of raising performance with team members is small step, incremental feedback based coaching, using the feedback sandwich.*

Using the feedback sandwich

The Feedback Sandwich is the most effective tool a coach or leader can use to gain incremental improvements in performance.

Using the feeling of personal motivation and the power of the unconscious mind, a well-structured, fluent feedback sandwich can be delivered in a matter of seconds. The embedded performance improvement is accepted by the other person's unconscious. It is possible that they have no conscious knowledge of the required improvement, but they will act on it.

Use this once a week to gain 50 or more, small performance improvement a year.

ALWAYS prepare the sandwich BEFORE delivery.

Once you get the hang of this, use it very regularly.

How to prepare your feedback sandwich

Deliberately observe your staff in the normal working environment. Keep notes (a journal really helps—one page or section for each staff member). Make a note of specific things they are doing well. Whilst observing, make a note of what they are doing well overall within their job, position, daily exchanges and activities.

For each sandwich, you want one (that is "1", "ONE", singular) specific action or behaviour that would improve their performance in the job.

It will be very beneficial to know what is important for each member of staff. Make no assumptions . . . ask them.

One of the easiest ways to do this is to ask them what they did at the weekend (or their time off work). Usually, not always, but usually, people do things in their time off that truly matter to them. Some will tell you what they did in chronological order, most will tell you the most important thing first. Make notes (later) of the specific words they used. For example:

- "I went shopping with my family" is not the same as "I went shopping with the wife and kids".

In the first, the important word is "family". To the second the word "family" may link, in their mind, to their entire family who are not really that important. "Wife and kids" might mean "family" to you, but to them it's a different thing and has a different importance in their life . . . a different value. In these same examples, you might ask "do you enjoy shopping?" then you could find out if they do or they do so because of obligation, promise or whatever . . . you've just found out that 'obligation, promise or whatever' is important to them.

- Do this every week—it will help you understand what is truly most important for these staff, and make them realise that you genuinely care about them.
- Keep a note of the values and the specific words—these make powerful garnish for your sandwich!

So now you have a list of specific things they have done well, specific improvements and words that symbolise what is important for them in their life.

- Now we can make the sandwich.

The format is this:

3 specific things you have done well, AND one thing to improve AND overall what you have done well. Use one or more of their own value words ("family" or "wife and Kids" within the sentence.)

Why it works

When someone tells you specific things you have done well, you know at least two things:

1. This person (boss, coach, parent) cares for me and,
2. that you have taken the time to observe what they do well.

At this point, receiving this feedback is positively motivating—especially when including suitable words that symbolise personal value.

Your motivation begins to drop by the third thing done well because you are anticipating the "but".

You, though, **do not use the word "but"**, you use the word **"and"**. (The word "but" emphasises the words after it and you do not want that.)

Now, you fluently go straight into the one thing to improve AND, fluently, go straight into the overall you are doing well.

At this point you have delivered the sandwich and STOP TALKING.

- No extras.
- No additional improvements.
- No final "but". STOP TALKING.

Now wait. They may ask for clarification, in which case, give any further specific evidence.

If they don't thank you. Thank them. Move on.

Trust this process. It works.

Feedback Sandwich Template http://gainmore.net/wbt-feedback

What's better today?

"What's better today?" John Kenworthy

What's Better Today? is both the singular most powerful thing you can do to change your own life and a whole lot of fun you can have with other people.

When you are asked to review your own performance it is more than 85% likely that you will focus on the negative aspects. You are well aware of the things that you do less than well.

If I asked you about what happened this week. You could easily regale all the negative things about work, your boss, your staff, your life. But what did you do this week that was good?

The world is filled with bad news. Things not going as well as they could—whether it's the economy, a scandal, a disaster. Good news rarely hits the headlines. In the same way, criticising ourselves is easy. Edifying (building up) ourselves truthfully is more difficult.

And it is important that you are truthful to yourself. This is not that great work of fiction you create when you apply for a new job. It's the things in your life that are better today than they were yesterday.

So what's better today? Tell me three things that are better today than they were yesterday for you.

Struggling?

Most people do, and I wish you could see your face as you tried to answer it.

So try this instead: Ask yourself two questions:

1. **What did you learn?**
2. **What did you enjoy?**

Now, you're getting somewhere. Simply use "what's better today?" as shorthand for these two questions.

If you would like to have some fun with this, the next person you meet today ask them "what's better today?"

It's common practice to greet people with variations of "How are you?" Most of the time you'll hear "OK" or "Good, thanks". Occasionally you get an organ recital: "Well, my legs been playing up and my back is aching, my tummy was upset and I have a headache . . ." Did you really want to know? There are many people you know who readily snatch defeat from the jaws of victory.

Instead, greet everyone with "What's better today?" Watch the response. Encourage them with the two questions if needed (What did you learn yesterday? What did you enjoy yesterday?) Keep doing it, people around you will look forward to seeing you. You will light up the room when you walk in. People will be drawn to you as a positive light in an otherwise dark world. And you'll feel good. You will be one of the few who is always snatching victory from the jaws of defeat.

Self-review

On a daily basis. Ask yourself "what's better today?". Note down 3 things (or more) that you enjoyed or learned or things you did to change AND 1 thing you want to improve AND overall what you are doing well.

Write it down. And speak it to yourself.

You are giving yourself a feedback sandwich. Nourishment for your learning and growth.

Write it down in your journal daily. Go through it once a week, then once a month, then once a quarter, then once a year. When you do this remember to keep ACTionable notes:

> A—**Apply**—something you want to apply or continue applying in your life
> C—**Change**—something you want to change
> T—**Teach**—something you want to or should teach others

This will re-affirm your learning and growth and show you when and how things actually changed for you . . . then you can teach others what you did for them to learn and grow. Maybe even write your memoirs.

If you take nothing else from this book. Take this please. Test it out this week. Just one week and see what happens.

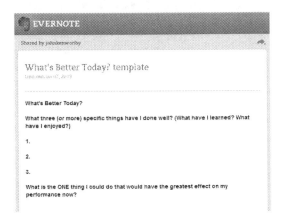

What's Better Today? http://gainmore.net/wbt-template

PART THREE

WRAPPING UP

Part Three—Wrapping Up

Part three of this field-guide is the oft-neglected but very important "wrapping up" stage of coaching.

Here we will consider and learn how to review the coaching and your achievements and learn how to acknowledge another person's contribution. If you have ever complained that you are not being recognised for your efforts or anyone had ever said that of you . . . then this is a key learning in itself.

Finally, we'll summarise the closure of this stage of your learning and growth as you enter the beginning of the next stage in continuing this journey.

Evaluation of process

"It takes twenty years of hard work to become an overnight success." Diana Rankin

How do you measure the effectiveness of coaching?

This is an issue that plagues the coaching profession, indeed it plagues training and development of any sort including school education. I wrote another book on Evaluating the Effectiveness of Training and Development based on my Doctoral Thesis if you are especially interested in this aspect.

When you invest in anything you want a return on your investment. Whether you are investing money, time, effort, energy, skills, knowledge, and resources. In this world we expect to gain something that we regard of greater value than the input. I mentioned the Motivation Triangle in the chapter on "Motivation to change". Well this is where we evaluate the achievement of the objectives.

Why is it so difficult to evaluate coaching effectiveness?

When we embark on a learning and growth journey there are many benefits we gain, but most are unsuitable for measurement.

If you set out to achieve a specific goal (that was genuinely SMART) you will know if you have achieved it or not.

There are times when you (and your coach) need to establish suitable metrics that will both help you monitor your progress and be suitable for evaluation. Some of the metrics will be a direct measure of achieving your goals and will be specific to each individual, but here are some examples to help your thinking on the matter.

- In sales: revenue, closings, funnel progressions, units shipped, customer sign ups
- In fitness: minutes of exercise, miles ran, visits to the gym, push-ups, weight, healthy meals
- In career building: resumes sent, interviews had, networking connections made
- In management: minutes in meetings, milestones met, team performance
- In leadership: team members performance, number of coaching or mentoring sessions held, number of staff who can state and explain the organisation objectives, number of feedback sandwiches given, time spent in own development, number of journal entries.
- In personal relationships: friends called, compliments given, evenings out, dates gone on, thank-you notes sent, invitations made
- In personal habits: minutes of walking, cigarettes smoked, time spent relaxing

Metrics that are regular updates to progress are extremely effective in evaluating the effectiveness of your growth and development. You may also consider using a pre and post coaching assessment.

My own clients for leadership coaching take an assessment at the beginning of their coaching and another at the end of their coaching engagement. This provides a tangible and useful measure of manifest leadership behaviour changes. Of course, not all can always be directly attributed to the coaching alone, but I ask my clients to estimate, for themselves, how much is attributed to their coaching and how much to the environment, for example.

ROI

Measuring the return on investment is not always easy though it is possible. Giving all investment a monetary value, your time investment as well, and then measuring the gain from your coaching—again given monetary value should show a positive return.

There seem to be very few coaches who encourage such evaluation. If you want to achieve tangible results from your coaching though, you should find one who does. You should certainly evaluate it yourself.

Subjective evaluation

It is very helpful to evaluate how you think and feel about your coaching as well as having harder measures. Some questions to help guide your consideration of this:

1. What do I think of my coach/mentor?
2. What is working well and why?

3. Is there anything that can be improved?
4. Are we communicating effectively?
5. How can we improve the communication?
6. Can we optimise the time we spend together?
7. What changes should we consider making so that things work better?
8. What are we spending too much time or too little time on?

By clear evaluation of your growth and development, you can provide useful feedback to your coach and ensure that you get what you need from the relationship. Remember, what gets measured, gets done.

Metrics

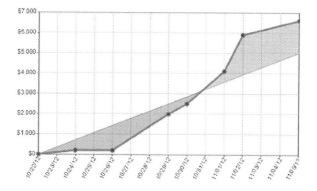

Whatever your coaching objectives, self-track one or two things that are important with Metrics.

Maybe you already know exactly what you should track, or maybe you need to just ask yourself what's something you'd like to work on.

Plan to track it for at least two weeks, it doesn't even have to be something you're being coached on directly. Set a target: something you are trying to work up to or get below.

One of the main reasons I use coachaccountable with my clients is the ease and usefulness of keeping metrics.

Create a Metric   X

Name: WBT Journal Entries

Unit of measure: Journal En

Date Span: Starting today   for 2   months , i.e. until 15/6/13

Frequency: I want to enter/track the value of this metric on an arbitrary basis

Target: I've got target values to aim for
- starting at 0   Journal Entry
- and ending target 51   Journal Entry, i.e. 1   Journal Entry every day
- The goal is to meet or exceed the target value
- Please record 0 Journal Entry as my value for today

Data Entry: Numbers entered will be...
- absolute. 3 means 3.
- incremental. 3 means "3 more than the last entry"

Reminders?   That would be great. Please...
- send Tarry a reminder at 12:00am via email
- when he hasn't entered a value in days

(Create) Close

You might use a to-do list or a simple calendar entry, a piece of paper or a spreadsheet. The tool is not as important as doing it.

What I do like with coachaccountable is it keeps my own metrics highly visible and keeps all my clients metrics up front.

The email reminders, especially in that 'red' spot, are excellent 'nags' to follow through with promises made to yourself and keeps you accountable.

Whichever system you use for keeping your metrics, make sure you keep them.

What gets measured gets managed.

Acknowledgement of contribution

*"Generosity is giving more than you can, and pride
is taking less than you need." Khalil Gibran*

One of the most common 'complaints' I hear about bosses is: "I'm
not recognised for my work". There is a major issue with this:

Being recognised by others is a value that is completely outside
of your control—it may happen, it may not. You cannot cause
someone else to recognise you or your contribution.

The only thing you can choose to do is to recognise others and
show your appreciation to them using their preferred method of
being appreciated. And yes I do mean showing the other person
your appreciation, and hence recognition, in the way they both hear
and understand that you have done so.

Gary Chapman at Paul White[1] have identified that there are five
languages of appreciation at work and each of us has a primary and
often a secondary way that we hear and understand for what it is. If

---

[1]   http://www.appreciationatwork.com/

someone uses the 'wrong' way for us, it's possible that we do not even notice it. In other words, someone could be recognising you, but because they are using the 'wrong' language for you, you do not hear or realise that they have done so.

Let me share an example of one husband and wife entrepreneurial couple who had set up a business together and had moderate success. The wife complained to her business mentor that she was 'fed up' because her husband never recognised her contribution to the business. On discussing this with the husband, he was shocked and a little frustrated because he was sure that he regularly thanked her and told her what a great job she was doing and lamented that she never told him that he was doing great . . .

The problem was simple, the husband's primary language of appreciation was 'words of affirmation'—he liked to be told that he was appreciated and consequently, that's how he showed his appreciation to others. His wife, on the other hand, wanted him to show it through him bringing the coffee, "at least once in a year" and to help her with the book-keeping at the end of month. She liked to be appreciated with 'acts of service'. Indeed, that was also how she showed her appreciation to her husband.

It wasn't that they were not recognising each other's contribution, just that they used their own language to show it rather than the other's language.

I strongly recommend that you find our your own preference, and the preferences of the people closest to you as well as your colleagues, your boos and your coach's.

The five languages of appreciation in summary are:

1. **Words of affirmation**—words spoken or written to affirm or encourage
2. **Acts of service**—Assisting someone with a task or working alongside someone to help them
3. **Tangible gifts**—Giving someone something they like and showing thought (rather than monetary value)
4. **Physical touch**—Whilst less important in the workplace than at home, this is the high-five congratulations or the literal 'pat on the back'—used only appropriately, touch can go a long way to show that you appreciate someone.
5. **Quality time**—focused personal attention with someone or simply 'hanging out'

Which of these do you like to receive? Which one does your boss like? If you honestly think you are not being recognised by your boss, I can guarantee that they are different. Now your job is to deliberately show them your appreciation by using their preferred language and recognise yourself.

If you have been working with a coach or a buddy on your learning and growth journey it's a powerful and kind thing to acknowledge their contribution.

Most coaches that I know have a fundamental personal driver to make a difference in the lives of others. We all know in ourselves that we have helped but the biggest reward you can offer your coach is to acknowledge their contribution . . . using, of course, their preferred way of being appreciated.

One of my own great moments in life was when someone I had chatted with years previously saw me again at a networking event. We said hello and then he told me that I had shared with him a story about being aligned to your goal using the metaphor of sailing and that he wanted to tell me that he still vividly remembered that moment when he had his big "aha" and changed his life. This wasn't even a client, just someone I had met once. But when he showed his appreciation to me (words of affirmation) I glowed inside and carried that feeling with me.

Use the Feedback sandwich template to provide feedback to your coach or buddy.

Closure and celebration

"Our ambition should be to rule ourselves, the true kingdom for each one of us; and true progress is to know more, and be more, and to do more." Oscar Wilde

Within a structured coaching programme, there is invariably a beginning and an end. However, some couples may decide to end the relationship ahead of the formal closure when the objectives have been reached or when the relationship has run out of steam or when it needs to be terminated due to unforeseen circumstances. Some relationships on the other hand continue even after the programme has ended. Once again it is up to coach/coachee to agree on this.

A more formal review should take place at the end of the programme, irrespective of whether the goals have been achieved or not. This is an opportunity to reflect on the results, celebrate successes, recognise learning. The important thing is that the relationship ends with positive feelings on both sides.

The end of the programme does not mean the end of the relationship. Many couples continue working together, meeting perhaps less frequently and more informally.

Very often it is at this point that many coachees consider passing on the knowledge and skills they gained by becoming coaches and entering into a new relationship.

The closure phase is both the ending and the beginning. You are ending the formal coaching relationship and beginning of the next stage of your development.

During your coaching engagement, an effective coach will ensure that you are equipped, enabled and empowered and will never do anything to make you feel dependent.

As your coaching draws to a close, you should have a plan of action going forward that continues your learning and growth. At this time, review your action plan and, as needed make changes or go through the entire cycle again.

A useful way for you to hold a closing briefing is the following guide:

1. Achievement of Objectives

This may already be clear to you, but it is worth reviewing the achievement of your coaching objectives. Here, you review the goals that both you and your coach agreed at the beginning of your relationship.

- To what extent did you reach your goal(s)?

- Using a scale from 0 to 10? (0 meaning no progress at all, 10 meaning goal(s) completely reached), how would you assess your achievement of your objectives?

The purpose, at this stage, is to focus attention on any part short of 10 and ask:

- What specifically is it that you did not accomplish?
- And, what has your coaching contributed to the progress made (maybe you started at 2 on the scale and now have reached a 7):
- In what ways did the coaching help you make the progress you have made?

Moving ahead

- What can you do to continue learning and growing from say a 7 to an 8?
- What specifically helped you change in your behaviour?
- What do others perceive in this regard?

2. Coaching Success

Reflect now on the success of the coaching itself:

- What three key insights you have learned?
- What specifically are you doing differently now?

3. Coaching Process

Also reflect on the coaching process itself:

- How satisfied are you with your coaching experience?

- What in the process would you like to see changed?
- Would you commit to this coaching process again? If so, why? If not, why not?
- Would you recommend this coaching process to others? If so, why? If not, why not?

4. Feedback by the coachee

And give your coach useful feedback (best in a feedback sandwich) and potentially including:

- Give honest and candid comments (not just compliments).
- Express your appreciation for your coach's trust and guidance (using their preferred language).
- Review the "successful" as well as the challenging and difficult moments in the coaching process.
- Reflect on your own role as coachee: Looking back, what would you have done differently?
- Address unsettled issues and open topics you may need to work on in the future.
- Suggest some kind of follow-up on your commitments
- Bring official closure to the coaching process.

ABOUT THE AUTHOR

Dr John Kenworthy is a **Professional Leadership Caddy** for Leaders who want to achieve greater success in their career, business and life.

He enables and supports you with the right tools and techniques at the right time so that you can align your skills, mindset and behaviour to realize your goals and dreams.

A Professional Leadership Caddy uses the approach that works best for you whether as coach, mentor, teacher, trainer, expert or shepherd so that you are truly empowered.

See our website at www.whatsbettertoday.com for more details

"What's better today?"

This is John's mantra. Every day he asks himself and everyone he meets. And it sums up his approach to leadership coaching and mentoring. It's also the title of his best-selling leadership book "What's Better Today? How to Grow and Learn into the Leader You Can Be".

John's mission is to help you achieve positive change enabling you to realize personal success in business, career and life.

John has a doctorate in leadership development from Henley Business School in the UK and has created a powerful leadership assessment tool, GAPPS4, the GAINMORE(TM) Advantage Potential to Performance System and his unique leadership development program, The GAINMORE(TM) Golf Leadership Challenge.

John is English by birth and now a Singapore citizen. He has lived in Singapore this past 18 years having worked and lived around the globe.

Originally a chef by trade, John puts his leadership 'nouse' down to his time in the kitchens.

> *During a single meal time, a chef faces every leadership and management issue that most other jobs barely see in a month. Add on the stress, the heat, the pressure and the instant feedback if you get it slightly wrong . . . you learn to think on your feet, take charge and make sure that the team is with you all the way. If you didn't learn how to be better, you'll find out soon enough . . . it all starts again in 1 or 2 hours!"*

> *So how does cooking relate to coaching?*

> *I am so glad that you asked . . . My templates and writing are my recipes My clients, their issues, their goals and dreams are my ingredients My skill is what makes the result acceptable or awesome*

John still cooks, but for pleasure.

Deeply loved, highly favoured and greatly blessed.

RESOURCES

All of the templates and resources referred to throughout these chapters are freely available for your personal use through our website at http://wbtbook.whatsbettertoday.com

You do need to register on the site to access all the resources.

What's Better Today? The Book Register here
http://gainmore.net/ wbt-register

- **Register**—http://gainmore.net/wbt-register
- **Login**—http://gainmore.net/wbt-login
- **Am I ready for coaching? Assessment**—
  http://gainmore.net/wbt-ready
- **Comparing Coaching, Mentoring, Counselling and Managing**—http://gainmore.net/wbt-compare
- **Motivation to Change Template**—http://gainmore.net/wbt-mtc
- **I Colour I Listen—Developing Active Listening Skills**—
  http://gainmore.net/wbt-icolour
- **Coaching Style Indicator Assessment**—http://gainmore.net/wbt-style
- **Mindset Diagram**—http://gainmore.net/wbt-mindset

- **Changing from Fixed to Growth Mindset**—Exercise—http://gainmore.net/wbt-change
- **Who does what checklist**—http://gainmore.net/wbt-check
- **Coaching Objectives Checklist Questions**—http://gainmore.net/wbt-obj
- **Coaching Agreement template**—http://gainmore.net/wbt-agree
- **Pre-Engagement Profile**—http://gainmore.net/wbt-pre
- **Who's your caddy?**—http://gainmore.net/wbt-caddy
- **SWOT template**—http://gainmore.net/wbt-swot
- **PEST Template**—http://gainmore.net/wbt-pest
- **SMARTening up my goals template**—http://gainmore.net/wbt-smart
- **SWING outcome setting**—http://gainmore.net/wbt-swing
- **Planning for growth**—http://gainmore.net/wbt-growth
- **Opportunity analysis template**—http://gainmore.net/wbt-oa
- **Values and anchors**—http://gainmore.net/wbt-values
- **Rocket ship for life**—http://gainmore.net/wbt-rocket
- **Creative and Survival Cycle Diagram**—http://gainmore.net/wbt-cs
- **Personal motivations for growth**—http://gainmore.net/wbt-motiv
- **Personal motivations template example**—http://gainmore.net/wbtmotiv-ex
- **Prioritization template**—http://gainmore.net/wbt-prior
- **Prioritization template example**—http://gainmore.net/wbt-prior-ex
- **Action Plan**—http://gainmore.net/wbt-plan
- **Feedback Sandwich template**—http://gainmore.net/wbt-feedback
- **What's Better Today?**—http://gainmore.net/wbt-template